Alcohol Lied to Me... Again: Get Back on the Wagon & Regain Control of Your Drinking

By Craig Beck

Published by Craig Beck Media Limited 2003-2018

www.craigbeck.com

www.StopDrinkingExpert.com

Alcohol Lied to Me... Again!
Copyright Viral Success Limited

This book reflects the personal experience of the author. It is not intended as a substitute for professional assistance, but describes a program to be undertaken only under the supervision of a medical doctor or other qualified healthcare professional. The preceding is copyright of Craig Beck Media, a trading division of Viral Success Limited 2003 – 2018.

Hypnosis reprogramming tracks mentioned in this book are available to download from
www.stopdrinkingexpert.com

Chapters

Introduction

The book 'Alcohol Lied to Me' has helped tens of thousands of people get back in control of their drinking thanks to its unique and simple to follow message.

But alcohol is the most devious and deceptive drug on planet earth and occasionally people fall back under its spell. This journey backwards virtually always starts with the same sentence being uttered: 'Surely just one drink won't hurt'.

Just one drink... it seems such an innocuous action that it couldn't possibly cause any substantial drama to unfold. In reality it is the same as hoping to take just one little step off a cliff. It's only one seemingly insignificant step but the consequences are rapid, irreversible and severe. Both events start off an unstoppable series of events.

In Alcohol Lied to Me... Again, Craig gives you the tools to once again break the cycle of alcohol addiction. You will discover why this relapse can be a good thing and how you use it to ensure you stay sober for the rest of your life.

If you have started drinking again... this book will guide you quickly back to a happy and fulfilled life, completely free from the misery of alcohol.

Craig also offers personal support and a series of unique tool to help you stop drinking alcohol in his online club – which has helped many thousands of people to quit and stay quit:
www.stopdrinkingexpert.com

Chapter One – What have you done?

There are three reasons why you may have bought this book. Firstly and most likely is, that having stopped drinking with 'Alcohol Lied to Me' or via the Stop Drinking Expert website you mistakenly believed that 'just one little drink' wouldn't do any harm. Now you find that your drinking is as prolific as ever and you are waking up every morning feeling terrible again.

The second most common reason for buying this book is your memories of all the pain and misery that alcohol caused you have started to fade and you are starting to feel conflicted. You still see all of your friends consuming their social poison and you are wondering if you could perhaps have the occasional drink.

And finally the third possibility is that you have incorrectly assumed this is the action pack sequel to the first book, the one where alcohol comes back and give my ass a good kicking all over the place. If you fall into this third category, I thank you for buying the book and respectfully suggest you prepare yourself for disappointment.

I am going to assume that you have already stopped drinking using my first book and that you managed to remain sober for a fair period of time. You are here because you are either strongly tempted to drink again or you have already made the mistake of assuming that 'just one drink won't hurt'.

Again I will start a journey with you by telling you that you are not alone. Do not despair just because you fell off the wagon. You are not weak willed, inadequate or stupid for making this mistake. Alcohol is the most powerfully deceptive drug on planet earth. You weakened its hold over you by quitting the first time around but you can't kill it. Alcohol will never change; it will never get less harmful or be able to be controlled. Every time you go back to it, the outcome will be the same. It will smile nicely, tell you it loves you and then immediately try to kill you.

A lot of people, who start drinking again having stopped with my help, find themselves in a panic. Nothing had worked to control their drinking until they found my books and websites. When they start drinking again they get suddenly very worried that even the thing that saved them is flawed and powerless against alcohol. They start to consider that they are profoundly unfixable and broken beyond repair.

None of this is true and is merely the drug twisting the knife and striving to complete the level. Alcohol wants you to return to your old drinking patterns but it also wants you to accelerate them exponentially, until you die. Why, you may ask? Because that is what alcohol does, it is its reason to be. Your relationship with booze is similar to the relationship between the frog and the scorpion:

One day, a scorpion looked around at the mountain where he lived and decided that he wanted a change. So he set out on a journey through the forests and hills. He climbed over rocks and under vines and kept going until he reached a river.
The river was wide and swift, and the scorpion stopped to reconsider the situation. He couldn't see any way across. So he ran upriver and then checked downriver, all the while thinking that he might have to turn back.

Suddenly, he saw a frog sitting in the rushes by the bank of the stream on the other side of the river. He decided to ask the frog for help getting across the stream.

"Hellooo Mr. Frog!" called the scorpion across the water, "Would you be so kind as to give me a ride on your back across the river?"

"Well now, Mr. Scorpion! How do I know that if I try to help you, you wont try to kill me?" asked the frog hesitantly.

"Because," the scorpion replied, "If I try to kill you, then I would die too, for you see I cannot swim!"

Now this seemed to make sense to the frog. But he asked. "What about when I get close to the bank? You could still try to kill me and get back to the shore!"

"This is true," agreed the scorpion, "But then I wouldn't be able to get to the other side of the river!"

"Alright then...how do I know you wont just wait till we get to the other side and THEN kill me?" said the frog.

"Ahh...," crooned the scorpion, "Because you see, once you've taken me to the other side of this river, I will be so grateful for your help, that it would hardly be fair to reward you with death, now would it?!"

So the frog agreed to take the scorpion across the river. He swam over to the bank and settled himself near the mud to pick up his passenger. The scorpion crawled onto the frog's back, his sharp claws prickling into the frog's soft hide, and the frog slid into the river. The muddy water swirled around them, but the frog stayed near the surface so the scorpion would not drown. He kicked strongly through the first half of the stream, his flippers paddling wildly against the current.

Halfway across the river, the frog suddenly felt a sharp sting in his back and, out of the corner of his eye, saw the scorpion remove his stinger from the frog's back. A deadening numbness began to creep into his limbs. "You fool!" croaked the frog, "Now we shall both die! Why on earth did you do that?"

The scorpion shrugged, and did a little jig on the drowning frog's back.

"I could not help myself. It is my nature."

Then they both sank into the muddy waters of the swiftly flowing river.

Alcohol is out to kill you, no matter what you do or how little your involvement with it.

Would you advise the frog to carry fewer scorpions across the river, perhaps limiting the activity to the weekends only? Or would it be much more logical that he never offers a ride to something that wants to kill him stone dead.

It is entirely natural for you to be feeling depressed because you have started drinking again. I give you permission to feel angry, despondent and disappointed in yourself and even me and my books – that didn't work! You have a license to hold your own personal pity party but let me tell you that permission expires at the end of this opening chapter. There is no value in beating yourself up about this event, grieving for your loss of sobriety or pointing the finger of blame somewhere.

Alcohol is a confidence trickster of unbelievable prowess. It is his job to scam you and he is relentless in the pursuit of that goal. Is it not true that if you were pickpocketed in the street one day, for a long time after the event you would be hyper vigilant, to guard against a repeat occurrence. However, if after a few years of being super cautious no further attempts to steal from you were made, wouldn't you lower your guard a little?

That is all that has happened... like sucker punch thrown by a boxer. You let your guard down and took a hit straight to your chin. In life, getting knocked down is inevitable. Getting back up is the choice!

The silver lining is this: maybe one of the best things to ever happen to you. The dark magician has fooled you again; it's a painful lesson. A mistake I know you are going to be much less likely to make again in the future. We develop and grow directly by learning from our failures. With this book as your guide you are about to sharpen your sword, strengthen the defenses and once again go back to war with the old enemy. But something significant has changed and swung the scales in your favor. You re-enter the field of conflict with your battle scars on show. You are an older and much wiser warrior this time around and naivety has been replaced by knowledge.

Your pity party license is officially revoked! We have a battle to win, so let's get started.

Chapter Two - David Blacksmith

Since the day you were born, everything that alcohol has told you is a lie. Everything that society believes to be a benefit is a lie and everything your drinking friends believe about alcohol is a lie.

Technology is rapidly progressing and at the time of writing this book, developers for the Intel Corporation have just released their first 72-core central processing unit. You don't need to be a computer nerd to grasp that this is a powerful step forward. This is an advance in technology so grand that will enable development of computers operating at breathtaking speed.

Despite the public fanfare of the announcement and the glitzy Hollywood style showcase that will no doubt herald the mainstream arrival of this computer chip... scientists have still only succeeded in creating something with a fraction of the power of the human mind.

When they transport that little computer chip to the red carpet launch party, it will be carefully packed into an airtight container, and placed inside a temperature controlled, anti-static environment. Only trained experts will be allowed to handle the precious cargo and even they will be monitored to ensure they are treating it with the respect it deserves.

brain, mind, spirit

Yet, we the possessors of machines vastly superior to that tiny new chip fling our contraption around like it is indestructible. We pour poison into our machine on a daily basis in the name of being social and then the next day we ignore the warning signs that we are causing serious harm to our mind and its container.

I am not going to waste our time going into what perfectly hideous ailments and diseases that alcohol causes. I am not going to bore you by telling you how many brain cells you destroy with every mouthful of the stuff you have been consistently knocking back for years or decades. Why? Because you are an intelligent and informed human being and you already know everything that I can tell you about the harm alcohol does. You have always known and it has never stopped you drinking so far, so I have no reason to assume a reminder of the facts will have the slightest bit of difference this time around.

Deep down we all know alcohol is nothing but attractively packaged poison. Our first encounter with it proved it. There is a reason that battery acid, bleach, cyanide and alcohol all taste disgusting. Human beings have evolved over millions of years, our success as a species is down to one thing 'the pure desire to survive'. Our body and mind have developed systems to keep us alive. We have the flight or fight response hard wired into our genetic make up and we have the ability to detect poisons before we ingest them, installed as a skill long before we are born.

To taste a poison, recognize it as such and then to force yourself to continue to consume it is as close to insanity as you can get. Alcohol is a learned addiction; we have to systematically ignore all the warning signs and even the appalling taste to literally force ourselves to get hooked on it.

In my book 'The Alcohol Illusion' I describe alcohol as the Dark Magician, who performs tricks to amuse us while with slight of hand he steals our health, money, relationships and most significantly our time on this planet.

Alcohol rewires your brain to ensure you keep using the drug. It achieves this over such a long period of time that you are completely unaware of it doing so. So when you stop drinking it takes an equally long time for your brain to start thinking like a sober person again. It is a very slow process of reawakening to life without a devious and dangerous drug continuously sloshing around in your body. Over the last five sober years of my life I have had a lot of time to reflect on how alcohol affected my behavior over the decades that I was a slave to it. My rose tinted glasses have long since been discarded and I can now observe other drinkers with more clarity and prospective than ever before. I might be free of it personally but I am still forced to watch people I love continue to drink, still trapped in the cycle. I now witness firsthand the denial and delusion proffered forth by all drinkers of this insidious drug. The same bullshit and illogical nonsense that I also used to preach at anyone who dared to question my drinking.

I describe alcohol as devious because of the slow but powerful way it traps the drinker into the loop of addiction. The first time you tasted alcohol was most likely the same way that I did... sneaking a sip of your father's booze when he asked you to be a good boy or girl and bring him a glass of it. I remember it like it was yesterday, I was eight years old and we had moved into our new home. It was so spacious and luxurious compared to the horrible apartment above a butcher's shop that we had squeezed ourselves into while the building work got underway on what would be our family home for the rest of my childhood years.

All the furniture was brand new and my parents still insisted on leaving the plastic sheeting on everything to preserve the newness for as long as possible. The air was thick with the strong but not unpleasant smell of the new carpets. My parents both came from humble 'working class' backgrounds and this house represented something very significant to them. It had stretched them to the limit financially and at times it seemed as though they had bitten off much more than they could chew. But yet, here they were at the end of the journey in their glorious new home. Bigger and more splendid than anything anyone on either side of the family had ever managed to achieve.

You could sense the pride oozing from my dad as he quite literally sat in his new throne, the king of his castle. He surveyed his kingdom and was happy. Such a moment in life should be savored and cherished which he did as he called out for his eldest son and I came running.

"Be a good lad and get your dad a whiskey from the new drinks cabinet in the dining room", he said with huge grin.

Having spent the last six months all squeezed into a tiny one bedroom flat you could tell the fact that we even had another room was such a novelty and a thrill for us all. Never mind that we had a dining room, a room just to eat in – wow the opulence of it all.

I ran to my mother and asked her for a whiskey glass. She opened a velvet-lined box, like something that you would expect to contain precious jewels. Opening it she passed me a glass so new that it still had a sticker on the side. It was so much heavier than it looked and I was quickly warned to be careful with it because it was 'Crystal', whatever that meant, certainly nothing significant to my eight year old self! But the warning in itself said that this was not just a guy having a drink this was some sort of very special ritual and both parents were acting like it was a big deal. I remember thinking when I drink my milk I don't have a special glass so what is so special about 'this whiskey' that it needs to be contained in something this extraordinary?

I carried the glass like it was a precious newborn baby bird resting in the palm of my hands. I walked into the dining room and flicked the light switch on, the new chandelier instantly filled the new decorated room with a warm light and I walked over to the drinks cabinet. The whiskey was already on top in a decanter equally as elegant as the glass I had waiting to pour it into. Also made of thick, expensive crystal with a giant glass stopper it was almost too heavy to lift, but I managed. Splashing uneven shots of whiskey into the glass until it was about a third full.

This was every small child's biggest challenge, not only to have the responsibility of carrying something so expensive but then to fill it with liquid too – I was running the gauntlet. This was perhaps the most important I had ever felt in my life, such pressure but oh what an honor. I remember feeling smug that there would be no way my younger brother Mark would be entrusted with such a task, he was a notorious spiller – this was way beyond him, a man's job if ever there was one.

Walking even more slowly and delicately than before with the heavy glass now containing this strong smelling but apparently magical liquid. I made it to the middle of the room before curiosity got the better of me; I nervously lifted the glass to my mouth. The first sensation to hit me was the smell, it was disgusting! It reminded me of the thick, black creosote that the groundskeeper at school used to mark out the football field with. Obviously, I then assumed the pleasure must come from the taste and not the aroma, for how could it... it was vile smelling stuff. Ignoring the smell and trusting in the hype I proceeded to take a large gulp of the golden water and waited for the magic to happen.

There was no magic... only fire! The burning liquid rushed through my young mouth and the most horrid medicine I had ever tasted assaulted my senses like a firework exploding in my mouth. The burning horribleness spread everywhere in milliseconds and quickly hit the back of my throat. I coughed and spluttered the liquid all over the new dining table and onto the brand new cream carpet. I gasped and held back the urge to cry but I had made enough noise to send my mother running from the kitchen. I was traumatized by the awful liquid but I also knew I was in big trouble because the firewater was strictly for grown ups. If they found out I had tried it I would be grounded for a month. With less than a second to spare I tipped the full glass of whiskey over myself, soaking my PJ's in the disgusting smelly liquid and started to cry, half to add credibility to my story and half because I really wanted to cry.

When my mum burst into the room I sobbed that I had tripped and spilt my father's whiskey. Once she realized I was not hurt her attention turned to her new carpet and I was ordered off to bed as she furiously dabbed at the liquor stains, which now were speckled across the new floor.

I tugged off my wet PJ's and threw them in the wash and lay on my bed wondering why on earth grown-ups could enjoy that horrible stuff so much?

I wondered... How can people get addicted to something that tastes so bad?

This is the first layer of false protection that people believe they have against developing a problem with alcohol. Even children who grow up in alcoholic homes can taste the stuff and confidently declare 'I will never get hooked to alcohol like my Dad (or Mom) because it tastes horrible'. What they can't account for at this early stage is the power of alcohol to rewire your brain to believe all manner of crazy things that don't make the slightest bit of sense to the sober mind.

The objective of this book is to remind you that alcohol is not a friend, supporting you through a traumatic and

27

stressful life. Alcohol is your worse enemy, taking all the beauty and wonder out of your life and replacing it with trauma and stress.

If you stopped drinking previously with my book 'Alcohol Lied to Me' you already know all this. And so you may be wondering how you could fall for the same tricks and end up back with the Dark Magician in your life again?

The primary reason is what I called the fading effect of the Threshold event. Back when you stopped drinking the first time around, all the evidence of the damage alcohol was causing was painfully clear to see. Perhaps you were struggling financially, your health was sliding away quickly or your partner was all set to pack the bags and leave you.

Human beings are motivated by two primary elements. The need to gain pleasure and avoid pain, unfortunately the scales are not evenly balanced and we will do significantly more to achieve the latter than the former. This is why misery, greed and discontentment are rife within most of western society. We will often only go as far as is needed to stop the pain without carrying on in our endeavours to push through to the point of pleasure. Diets fail over and over again for this very reason alone.

The Story of Jenny Taylor

Jenny looks in the mirror and grabs hold of the new roll of fat that has slowly developed around her waist. She sighs and looks forlornly at the wardrobe full of clothes that no longer fit. Her weight and body size is making her miserable, but for the moment the pain is not enough to justify giving up the food she loves and associates with a lifestyle she believes herself worthy of. Her current mental assessment is that living without the fine dining, chocolate, cakes and weekend takeaways will be more unpleasant than ~~that~~ how she currently feels about her body.

The next day at work something happens that dramatically changes her opinion, as she steps out of the elevator and makes for her cubical she stops short and waits before turning the corner. She hears her name being mentioned in conversation and cocks her head to one side, listening to what is being said. A new intern is asking one of the sales staff who Jenny Taylor is because he has a package to leave on her desk. The salesman, who is rushing out the door on a client call, he is already ten minutes late for shouts over his shoulder 'cubicle 17, big woman, brown hair'!

Jenny's jaw drops open as she gets slapped around the face by the realization that people describe her as 'the big woman' of the office. In my weight loss book Fat Guy Friday this is what I call a threshold moment. This is a point in time when the pleasure/pain balance gets dramatically shifted. Suddenly the pain of being overweight and the associated low self-image becomes massively exaggerated and overtakes the other now insignificant pressure preventing the person from taking action.

Horrified by what she has just overheard, Jenny throws her fried chicken lunch in the garbage and the diet starts immediately. On the way home from work she stops off at the gym and signs up for a yearlong commitment to the dreaded treadmill (despite the fact that she hates the gym, but not quite enough to silence that statement 'big woman, brown hair'). Fitness centres tie you into fixed term deals because they know your current good intentions are going to last six to eight weeks at best. Then you will be banging on their door demanding that they stop debiting your account every month. Regular gym goers hate January because the treadmills and stationary bikes are clogged up with the New Years Resolution gang; thankfully by March most of them are gone. Although chances are good that they are still paying the club fees because ending a gym membership can sometimes be harder than getting a divorce.

The rabbit food replaces the pizza and Jenny Taylor drags herself to the gym daily for a whole month. That salesman gets at least a dozen evil looks a day as the echo of his description bounces around her wounded mind. Diet cereal for breakfast, salad for lunch and boiled fish for dinner... until one day the jeans that were once too tight slide over her hips. A delightful occasion for any dieter and the next day at work, back in her skinny clothes a few of her colleagues notice the weight loss and make pleasing noises in her direction. The motivational scales take another swing as the pain from the threshold moment dissipates and loses it leverage.

Within a week or so Jenny is allowing herself the 'occasional treat' and skipping the gym on days when she feels a little tired. Within a month she has started to resent the $70 a month the fitness centre takes out of her account, as it feels it is poor value for the odd time she actually makes it past the highway turnoff. It's not long before the pain of depriving herself of life's luxuries far outweighs the trauma of that now distant threshold event. The weight slowly returns until the cycle starts again.

This is what we call the yo-yo diet routine and it's why 95% people who go on a low fat, calorie restrictive diet not only put back on any weight lost, but also adds on average an additional 2-5 lbs.

If you had been a long time sober you might be baffled by how you could give up such a hard fought for victory by drinking again. Take heart that your stumble on the sober road was always very likely and some say even vital to your long-term success. As time moves on, everything changes. You body begins to heal itself, as it no longer has to deal with a daily injection of poison. Some of the aches and pains created by your addiction fade away and you start to sleep and recharge better than you have done in decades. The threshold event that brought you so much pain in the past is now just a distant memory and as such its power is significantly reduced. The only thing that stays the same during this entire process is alcohol. Alcohol is the constant that never changes, it always tastes bad, it always lies and it always wants to kill you.

Just because you don't drink any more doesn't mean you are protected from its lies. You still get to watch your family and friends consuming alcohol. You still have to listen to them all insist that it is a harmless social pleasantry. You still get to watch the TV commercials that portray drinkers as smart city executives and other such successful high flyers. You still have to get insulted by drinkers who see your abstinence as a threat to their own addiction. You get called boring and anti-social. Drinkers give you funny, distrustful glances when you order a soft drink instead of wine or beer.

You are not immune to the deceit of alcohol just because you choose not to consume it. You live in a world where 80% of the adult population are all habitually using a dangerous drug – how can you not be affected by that? The answer is you can't and neither was David Blacksmith.

David Blacksmith (named has been changed) slowly developed a serious drink problem over fifteen years. The drug very nearly won and achieved its ultimate goal. It took him to the brink of devastation, to the edge of bankruptcy, divorce and death. Nothing he tried to control his drinking worked, until he found my Stop Drinking Expert website. He has always been one of my most vocal fans, preaching my message to anyone who will listen – for no other reason than his own deeply ingrained gratitude.

I can't tell you how many emails and phone calls I have had over the years that started with 'David Blacksmith told me to get in touch with you... I have a problem...'. Then in 2013 they all stopped and David's name vanished from my inbox. No more Internet forum posts, no more virtual chats, no more emails – nothing but silence. The void that David left behind was instantly noticeable and I worried about him. I tried to track him down to make sure he was okay but my emails were ignored and my phone calls were sent straight to voicemail.

I am sure you have already guessed why. David, had started drinking again. Despite having wrestled himself from the jaws of total destruction and escaped by the skin of his teeth, he had willingly accepted an invite from the Dark Magician to one little game of chance. David believed the one sentence that always ends in devastation. The one little innocent sentence, which has been uttered a million times by recovering drinkers around the world. And has never once been found to be true.

"Just one drink won't hurt'.

That one sentence started all the pain and misery up again, like throwing gasoline on a smoldering ember.

David didn't start at the beginning of his addictive cycle; he jumped right back in at the point he left. With alcohol there is no rewind button and no stop button... there is only play and pause. The good news is you can live a happy and fulfilled life for the rest of your days with the pause button down but never with the play button engaged.

David's Story:

I won't bore you too much with my own person tale of alcohol induced destruction. The reason for the lack of detail is only because I believe that the reliving of our past mistakes doesn't achieve anything noticeably positive. No matter how gruesome and traumatic my story is, it will never feel as real and painful as your own personal battle with this devious drug. I will try to condense my tale into a digestible paragraph or two, purely to give my involvement in this book some context.

Like everybody else, I suspect, I never expected that I would be anything other than a normal social drinker. I occasionally joined my colleagues for a pint or two and every now and again woke up with the traditional hangover the morning after parties and work functions. I observed the unwritten rules of drinking such as; You must start drinking before noon when you are on holiday and of course it doesn't matter what time your departing flight is, a pint at the airport is almost as mandatory as it is to get a few good squirts of free aftershave (with no intention of buying any) on the way through duty free. There was nothing remarkable about my drinking and I am loathed to use the cliché but I really could take it or leave it.

Craig is right that it is the slow, devious way that the drug hooks us in that makes it so dangerous. I honestly don't remember the time when my drinking changed from something social to a coping mechanism. I have no recollection of when my drinking became a daily event rather than an occasional 'pleasantry'. All I can really remember is a staccato series of bad times that started to ring alarm bells that I was no longer in control of my drinking.

They started out with minor disappointments rather than dramatic tragedies. I started doing things that people described as 'not like David'. They were mostly small mishaps that I managed to cover up with a quickly constructed lie. The day I went to the pub for a quick lunchtime drink and ended up staying all day and missing my son's first ever school nativity. I never got to see him walk shyly onto the stage dressed as a wise man. I blamed my failure to attended on my arsehole of a boss, who had kept me working late and made me miss the performance. That was a priceless moment that alcohol stole from me, I never got to see how cute and adorable he looked on that stage. I tried to picture it in my mind but the guilt made it difficult.. I however, had no problem repeatedly imagining him scanning the audience for the proud, supportive faces of his mum and dad and finding an empty seat where I should have been.

My wife Amanda believed the lie and later that evening her anger and disappointment was aimed squarely at my boss. She was several times on the brink of ringing him and lambasting him for being so selfish and mean spirited. Obviously I had to prevent that happening at all costs and I found myself in an ever-expanding lie, all because I had preferred the company of a drug over my wife and child.

This may or may not be the beginning of my story, I can't remember. I know I could fill a book with endless dreadfully painfully things that happened as a result of me making equally poor choices, as alcohol continued to tighten its grip on me. I don't need to relive these stories because I know you have your own that would serve to make the point just as well, if not a whole lot better.

Instead I will skip forward five or six years to what I will call the beginning of the end.

In my twenties I had been earmarked as a bright rising star of the future in my chosen industry of financial risk assessment. By the time I turned thirty I was leading a team of fifteen and on a salary way beyond that anyone of my age had ever achieved in the history of the bank. If I was ranked anything lower than 'outstanding' in my annual performance review I assumed there had been a mistake. I was confident, focused and very good and what I did. My success had not gone unnoticed and I was assured that within five years I was destined for director level and the associated six figure salary was a given.

I never made director and at the age of thirty-nine I was sacked by the bank I had worked at since the age of twenty-four for gross misconduct. I had received several formal warnings for my time keeping, behavior and other assorted indiscretions. My annual performance reviews had struggled to creep above 'unsatisfactory' for many years and so I should have seen the bullet coming. But I didn't or at least I fooled myself into thinking I was doing nothing wrong, and it was the system that was failing, not me. This one event kicked over the first domino that would see my whole life fall apart.

I arrogantly declared to my friends and family that I was better than that bank and I would land on my feet sure enough. I declared that getting sacked would end up being the best thing that ever happened to me. This was all front and show, on the inside I was terrified and I remember the very same night locking myself in the bathroom and sobbing my heart out, using the running water to disguise my cries. I knew deep down inside that alcohol had broken me, I was no longer a man that ran on passion, determination and hard work but rather I had become a pointless machine that ran on poison.

What I discovered quickly was that being employed was the only thing preventing me from drinking all day as well as all night. Once this vital element was forcibly removed from my day-to-day life, I crashed into a drunken oblivion. We quickly fell into financial difficulties and despite Amanda's best efforts the house was taken from us less than a year later. I would be proud to say that this was the final wake up call and I got myself together shortly afterwards. Sadly this is not the case and I lost much much more than bricks and mortar before I found the bottom of the barrel.

I knew my drinking was out of control long before the damage started to appear in my personal and professional life. I tried to cut down more times than I can remember. I stopped for three months once, but it was three months of living hell – where everyday I had to force myself to avoid drinking. At the end of three months of torture, all it took to push me over the edge was another one of those 'unsatisfactory' performance reviews from my idiot boss. I stopped at the off license on the way home and told myself that my life sucked enough as it was without me removing the one genuine pleasure I had left. I bought a bottle of Jack Daniels and spent the evening drowning my sorrows.

Everything I tried to get my drinking under control failed. The GP was next to useless and when I told him how bad things had become he suggested I drink less. No shit Sherlock, I thought as I walked back to my car – completely out of ideas and hope. I decided the best way to deal with my depression was to drink myself into oblivion again.

In the September of that same year, Amanda packed her bags and took the kids to live with her parents in Coventry. The evening after she left, I remember sitting in the disgusting two bed flat we had managed to get after the house was taken and feeling the silence was all consuming. I was lonely and full of pain and regret, I decided to drink until the sensation went away. I sat on the sofa in my underwear, a glass of whiskey in one hand as I balanced the laptop on my knee and searched for ways to stop drinking.

I found Craig's website 'The Stop Drinking Expert' and I thought 'bullshit', this guy has no idea what I have been through. I was about to hit the back button when I noticed how he described alcohol. Some of the things I thought had been unique to my personal situation were being highlighted as 'common' tricks of a devious drug. I started to read more and for the next few nights I sat on that sofa (still with a glass of booze in my hand) and read about Craig's own destructive journey with alcoholism. I laughed out loud at some points, not because it was hilariously funny but he had also done some really ridiculous things just to desperately cling onto alcohol as a crutch to life's problems.

I was wondering where 'the cure' was supposed to come in when one night I noticed that at eleven o-clock I was still sober. I had drunk a fraction of what I usually would, it left me genuinely baffled and amazed. The next night I poured the whiskey but I ended up tipping it down the sink, shortly after the remainder of the bottle followed it.

I am not going to say it was completely painless, the next night I had a panic attack that I had thrown away the only thing that helped me deal with life. Additionally the stark reality of how far I had dropped and how squalid my living standards had become hit home like a armor tipped missile. But I took the supplements mentioned in the book and started the hypnosis programme he suggested and slowly I found that the grip alcohol had on me began to weaken, until it had no more strength than that of a new born baby.

At first my family and friends thought it was just another of my sober struggles. They fully expected me to fall off the wagon at any moment and continue my rapid decline into the depths of despair. When that moment never arrived and they witnessed the old David start to return, their faith in me also came back. My reputation in the financial sector was ruined but I was able to pull myself together enough to start my own business, which slowly began to thrive. Amanda came back and we moved into a new apartment. Still nowhere near what we had been used to when I was in banking, but while the granite work surfaces were missing and the en-suite bathrooms no where to be seen. Something else was also missing, alcohol was no longer a part of our lives. This turned an average suburban house into the first proper home we have ever had.

Holidays, many Christmases and birthdays passed and all without a single urge to celebrate any of them with the dreaded alcohol. Alcohol Lied to Me *had saved me from the brink of disaster. Without it I would probably not be here now. I became one of those evangelical ex-drinkers who can't keep themselves from preaching the way out of the misery. I told anyone and everyone about this website I had found and helping other people to free themselves of this poison started to feel nearly as good as rescuing my own family.*

As Craig explained, I did become his super stalker for a while. I was just so grateful for the hand he had reached out to pull me from the pit of despair I had fallen into. Everything was going so well, I was happier than I had ever been in my adult life. Amanda and the kids were beaming for ear to ear and I just couldn't believe how much energy I had, practically bouncing out of bed each morning. I had claimed that getting fired would be the best thing that ever happened to me, it turned out I was right. But I would never have dreamed how painful the process would end up being.

It had been nearly five years since I had touched a drop of the 'attractively packaged poison' as Craig calls it, I was sitting in the sunshine in a beer Garden in North London, having a working lunch. My client Brian had just collected his pint from the bar and sat down opposite me on the wooden picnic bench. As Brian was a new client, we made small talk and danced around the contract we were planning to sign that day. As I finished my orange juice and he knocked back the final mouthful of the freezing cold, golden liquid in his pint glass. He stood and said 'another one David, or perhaps something a little stronger'?

Brian had no idea of my history with alcohol, to him his question was an innocent everyday statement. For me, even though I had heard the very same question a thousand times over the years and never had any problem quickly saying a firm 'no thank you'. For some reason today was different, the question lingered in the air for a few seconds. I took in the scene around me, the dozens of people smiling and appearing to enjoy a harmless beer in the sunshine. And then I did it, I asked the one question of myself that was to begin the misery afresh. I said to myself 'Just one beer won't hurt' and I nodded my agreement at the suggestion.

As Brian walked to the bar my heart was racing, was I really going to drink the beer that would be soon placed in front of me? I was struck by a thousand conflicting thoughts, and I let alcohol lie to me once more. The dark magician jumped on my shoulder and whispered in my ear "Drink the beer or tell the new client that you are an alcoholic'... the choice is your Davey boy'.

Brian placed the foamy, golden pint in front of me and watched me suspiciously as I stared at it for an unnaturally long amount of time. Eventually, he stood up and said 'sorry did you want a bitter instead of lager'? I assured him I was fine and motioned for him to sit back down as I raised the poison to my lips for the first time in half a decade. As I tasted the beer I was delighted to discover it tasted disgusting. It was really sharp and unpleasant and I struggled to finish the pint.

On the tube on the way home I felt ten percent guilty as a result of the indiscretion but ninety percent relieved that the beer hadn't tasted amazing. I concluded that I really was cured and there was no way I could get hooked again because it tasted so vile. My joy and delight continued the next day when I had no desire to drink, indeed I went a full three days before I decided that now that I was cured I could have the occasional drink to be social. On the way home from work I stopped off at a pub and order a pint of beer and successfully had just one drink, before continuing my journey home. Stopping off at the shop on the way to buy some breath mints. This should have been a clear sign that the madness had already restarted. I was already trying to cover up my drinking and blocking out the screaming voice of my sanity that was trying to warn me of what was coming.

The next day something had changed, I still believed that I could have just have one drink, if and ▪when I so desired but I noticed that I was continually looking at the clock. Not to see if it was time to go home but to see if it was time to have my solitary social drink. I somehow managed to have one pint and head for home, but I no longer felt the confidence of a few days previous.

This pattern continued for a few weeks before Amanda said she was taking the kids to see her mum and dad for the weekend. My instant thought was … I am going to have a day to treat myself. I was going to get the new bond film on BluRay, a massive pizza and a bottle of Scotch and have an afternoon in front of the television that I never got chance to control normally.

The Dark Magician told me:

1. *Of course I would only have a couple of drinks. No need to worry about drinking the whole bottle – that would never happen.*
2. *I deserved it, I had been working hard and I needed a treat.*
3. *It's not a big deal, I was nowhere near my old levels and life was going along pretty damn good thank you very much.*
4. *I was stronger now, I could control it this time.*

I drank the whole bottle and woke up on the sofa in the early hours of the next morning. I was dehydrated and felt off the scale ill. I bagged up the evidence of my drinking and drove to the recycling center to make sure my secret stayed exactly that. When Amanda came home and found me moaning and complaining on the sofa I told her it was the dreaded man-flu.

The hangover kept me off the booze for a few days, but exactly like before, it wasn't long before I was trying to come up with reasons where it was okay to drink. Creating those silly rules to try and control the uncontrollable. Craig had already explained to me how the trick is done and yet here I was watching the magician perform the same routine and falling for it all over again.

You might wonder why I didn't contact Craig as soon as I started drinking again. There are several reasons for that aside from the deep shame and guilt that I was feeling. I was terrified that the only thing that ever worked in my battle with the booze had turned out to be a fraud. The Stop Drinking Expert had failed to cure me and now I was destined for an unstoppable decline back into the madness. Of course I should have seen that even this was just another alcohol lie, but when you are in the dark it's hard to see the way out.

It took me a few months of misery, lies and depression before I emailed Craig and explained what had happened. I expected him to be pissed off with me or to just ignore me as a failure. I didn't expect him to say 'don't worry it's a good thing'. He explained that relapse is a part of the journey but he doesn't mention that in the book because he doesn't want to give drinkers permission to fail.

We started talking about some of the new lies I had started to believe and the reasons for me drinking. Exactly as before, every single excuse I came up with to justify my return to alcohol he blew it apart with indisputable logic and common sense. We talked for a few hours and that was that... it really was that quick. Alcohol is gone from my life again and this time I have a new weapon in the war. I have been there and tried the 'just one drink' lie and I am here to tell you that it's nothing but one hundred percent, pure grade bullshit.

My message to you my friend is this... you are not broken and neither is the system. The first time you stopped drinking you were only allowed to progress to brown belt. You couldn't take the black belt training without a few more battle scars. So here you are at the dan grade stage and you are about to get stronger than you ever thought possible.

Like all drinkers David thought his story was unique. He believed that he was the broken one, the person who was so hooked that he was beyond help. Please trust me, the dark Magician knows a few good tricks but his act is limited and predicable. Its similar to the way Penn & Teller perform. They make their audience gasp in wonder and amazement at a mind-blowing illusion. Then they break all the rules of the magic circle and show you exactly how they managed to fool you. If they then repeated the trick, do you think you would still gasp in amazement? Probably not, because once you know how the illusion is done, it loses its power.

I see the exact same story with alcohol being played out all over the world. If you think you are the exception to the rule who can't be fixed then let me tell you. That is as silly as assuming that you are the only one who gets burned by fire.

What has happened to you is an entirely predictable response to the repeated consumption of a poison. If you pour itching powder into your pants you will get the uncontrollable urge the scratch the itch. If you rub chili powder in your eyes, it will hurt and they will turn red, while streaming tears to try and clear the irritant. If you drink an addictive drug – you will get addicted, it's really as simple as that. Stop making this personal, it's not. Alcohol doesn't care who you are or what you have to lose. Wealth, geography and social standing are an irrelevance; it only wants one thing, to kill you.

Believing that falling off the wagon is due to your terrible weakness as a human being is just another lie of the drug. Over the course of the rest of this book I am going to help you back onto the wagon by showing you that every other reason or excuse you can come up with to facilitate the continuation of your drinking is also nothing more than a big fat lie. We will start this journey together with the most common lie of all, 'I am only drinking to be sociable'.

Chapter Three - Moving Mackenzie to the movies

I do love the way the universe works. When I was writing Fat Guy Friday, my weight loss book, I just happened to get uncomfortably squeeze between two chronically obese men on a flight from Cyprus to the United Kingdom. When I was writing Alcohol Lied to Me, air travel once again threw me some inspiration when I accidentally upset a friendly airhostess. The lady in question was trying to give me free booze. She was quite confused by my refusal to accept such a wonderful free gift. As I sit here writing the sequel to that bestselling book, once again the universe has decided to put on a little show for me.

These days I have traded in the rain and gloom of England for the sunshine and warm blue sea of Larnaca, Cyprus. Larnaca is town of just under 80,000 inhabitants on the east coast of the island. The mentality of the local people is more like you would experience in a small village than a town or city. Everybody seems to know each other and we all tend to socialize at the same events.

Through the summer months a local rock band called Minus One play a free gig every Sunday afternoon for the locals. It feels like the whole of Larnaca makes its way down to Mackenzie beach and enjoys the music while sitting in the baking hot sunshine. Today was the last Sunday of the free concerts on the beach and my friends and I were all discussing what we are going to do on subsequent Sunday's now our usual entertainment had finished.

Eighty percent of the western world drinks alcohol and that stat is reflected in my friends. I only have one friend who doesn't drink. Natasha suggested that we start going to the movies on a Sunday instead. I thought it was a great idea, the weather would be cooling down soon and we could all meet up watch a movie and then go for a meal at one of the nearby restaurants.

To my surprise the idea was roundly declared to be a terrible one, but nobody would offer a reason as to why. It was only when our friend Sally (name has been changed) turned up looking terrible and complaining that she felt worse than she looked that I understood why the group didn't want to replace the bars of Mackenzie beach with the movie theatre.

Sally explained that she had been at a party the day before and they had started drinking at eleven in the morning. They continued to drink all day and all night, finally finishing the marathon session at five the following morning. The group universally congratulated Sally for her immense staying power and she took her bow accordingly. At this point I walked to the bar to get her a bottle of water, which I thought might ease her discomfort. I presumed that the 35c degree heat (95f), her obvious state of dehydration and the booming rock music were not doing her any favors.

As I placed the freezing cold bottle of water in front of her she smiled and said "Oh thanks love, but could you get me a large beer too – I am determined to kill or cure this hangover".

I have long since learned to bite my tongue; I smiled and said of course. I ignored the urge to point out that at no point in history has anyone been admitted to hospital with acute poisoning for the doctor to prescribe more of the poison that caused the problem in the first place. However, the rest of the group again agreed it was a sound plan and would probably work, if she forced the first pint of beer down.

Drinkers never fail to bemuse me with their logic but on this occasion it did cause a little light bulb to flash above my head. The reason the cinema was so roundly rejected by the group is there is no opportunity to drink alcohol in the local movie theatre. Our group claim to get together to be social but if you take away the drug our union falls apart.

When you take the opportunity to drink away from drinkers then life becomes miserable. So it is not so much that alcohol makes a party go with a swing but without it most people would feel uncomfortable and depressed without the opportunity to consume their drug. We know from studying other cultures that alcohol is not the reason social gatherings are fun. In the eastern world they have some of the most joyful celebrations, full of dancing and singing without a single drop of alcohol crossing anyone's lips.

Ignore the elegant packaging and carefully targeted brand positioning and you are left with the reality that alcohol is nothing more than the waste byproduct of decaying vegetable matter. It is not a smart liquid developed by NASA, just a basic waste product just like urine. Once you appreciate this fact then you must accept that it cannot change the way it affects the human body and mind. If alcohol really makes party more fun then it must do this every time. But I am sure that like me you have been to parties that are awash with booze and yet they have a terrible atmosphere and are so boring you spent the whole evening repeatedly glancing at your wristwatch and wondering if it had stopped working.

In the western world we have all agreed to buy into the lie that a party is not a party without hideous amounts of booze to help it flow. Alcohol is a mild anesthetic, so this theory actually makes no sense at all. If a spectacular celebration were arranged then surely it would be better if the guests were at the very least conscious. What is the point of decorating the function room, choosing a theme for the party and even paying for a popular band to play the music if the first thing you do is give all the guests an anesthetic so they can't really appreciate their environment?

Anesthetics are a godsend but are not needed to make a party go well. Only when administered by highly trained professionals in a medical setting are anesthetics a benefit. I was recently admitted to hospital for an operation and I was certainly glad of the opportunity to remove my consciousness while the work was carried out.

A slight genetic defect had caused my hip socket to overdevelop during childhood and the years of wear and tear since then have caused a rip to appear in the labrum around the joint. Until fairly recently this was an untreatable condition that would eventually lead to a full hip replacement. Thankfully advances in medical science and specifically keyhole surgery mean that the tear can now be repaired and the offending overgrowth of bone filed down to prevent further damage to the hip.

The operation is called a hip arthroscopy, which involves the leg being stretched until the hip dislocates. This is achieved with a contraption that looks quite similar to a medieval torture device, which was known as 'The Rack'. I knew far too much about the operation I was about to have thanks in part to YouTube and my over inquisitive mind. As a result I have discovered that information is not always power and often it's much better to remain completely uninformed, head in the sand ostrich style. As they say; you can't un-see things no matter how much you want to and there is no doubt this unnecessary curiosity helped turn me into an embarrassing, gibbering wreck on the day of my admission to Harrogate Hospital in North Yorkshire.

Thanks to a spinal block and general anesthetic I felt none of the torture my body was to be put through. A double whammy of pain preventing measures to ensure I neither felt anything during the operation itself or for eight to nine hours directly after it. Despite such comprehensive medical care I am afraid to say it did not prevent me acting like a complete big girl's blouse when I sat in the anesthetic room awaiting an epidural that would render me paralyzed from the waist down. A very desirable state to be in considering 'The Rack' was waiting on the other side of the swing doors at the opposite end of the room.

The nurses tried to calm me by asking questions about my day-to-day life. Trying to slow my panicky heart rate down by asking what I thought of the local football team's performance at the weekend. Ashen faced I tried my best to join in the distracting small talk but I was genuinely terrified about what was coming next. I can't imagine how I would have coped in those times before modern day medical procedures and drugs... oh the drugs, God bless those drugs!

If alcohol is a harmless bit of fun, why did naval doctors and Victorian surgeons reach for the rum and not something else?

The answer is Alcohol is not a harmless inert substance. Alcohol is indeed a mild anesthetic, a chemical that interferes with our brain chemistry until it cannot function as it was designed to. Of course when you are having your leg amputated you really need something a long way from 'mild' to take the edge off the procedure but it was all they had and so it was welcomed all the same.

Difficulty walking, blurred vision, slurred speech, slowed reaction times, impaired memory: all side effects of the drug we collectively declare to be nothing more than a social pleasantry.

Some of these impairments are detectable after only one or two drinks and quickly resolve when drinking stops. On the other hand, a person who drinks heavily over a long period of time may have brain deficits that persist well after he or she achieves sobriety.

Imagine if a chocolate bar was released to market today and shortly after it went on general sale it was found to have anaesthetic properties and if within days consumers were crashing their cars into each other, being admitted to hospital with an array of serious and sometimes fatal side effects. How long do you think this product would remain on the shelves? It would be banned in no time at all and the company behind it would be so comprehensively sued that they would surely go bust in a hurry.

Alcohol does all this and more, yet it remains on supermarket shelves around the world with a licence to be marketed as literally anything the drinking manufacturer desires. No other product has such freedom; alcohol can be portrayed as fun, sexy, aspirational and can even promise to make people like you more!

Imagine if a tyre company ran a TV commercial that claimed fitting your automobile with their new winter cross ply will make you more attractive to the opposite sex and lead to more success at work! This would be labelled as false advertising and deemed misleading to the general public! The commercials would probably never see the light of day and yet alcohol makes a never-ending array of erroneous promises that go unchallenged. The marketing of alcohol will one day be highlighted as the epitome of deceitful manipulation. It is a big factor in why so many drink and why you have had a problem with alcohol. We will talk about this in more detail later in the book, for now lets return to the hospital.

As I lay on the operating table waiting to be wheeled into theatre the anaesthetist reassured me that I would be asleep during the whole process. Sounds quite pleasant doesn't it? Sadly it's not true, anaesthetic does not induce sleep but rather a reversible coma. Cerebral activity is slowed down to something close to brain stem death, rendering the patient unconscious and completely unaware. There are no dreams to remember upon waking from a general anaesthetic, as the brain was not capable of creating anything so complicated.

If you drop a brick on your foot it will hurt like hell and probably break your bones. You can't chose to ignore this reality and claim that all it will do is tickle and make you skip around the room in a giddy mood. If you consume an anaesthetic it will dangerously interfere with the wiring in your head, but we do like to claim all sorts of nonsense to cover this fact up. We claim that alcohol makes us more fun to be around, gives us confidence and makes us more sociable. None of these claims can be true, the only thing alcohol does is make you stupid.

Stupidity is not a state to desire or to envy in others. When you play peak a boo with a baby, disappearing behind your hands and hiding from the child. The baby is genuinely shocked that you appear to have instantly vanished. When you re-appear from behind your hands, the delight on the baby's face is clear to see. This simple trick manages to fool the baby because he or she does not have the information or intelligence to understand that just because they cannot see you does not mean you have left the room.

In a small child this is considered cute and endearing but imagine if you met an adult who was so stupid that he also believed that if he couldn't see you then that meant you had miraculously vanished. This would be a long way from cute and we might even wonder if the person was a little mentally disabled.

People on alcohol believe much more ridiculous things than this. Many drunks are rushed to hospital each year having fallen from a great height, after the misguided belief that they could fly or jump from building to building like Spiderman. Alcohol causes stupidity that we incorrectly label as other more positive personality traits. You brain is highly evolved to communicate effectively with a wide range of people. If you met someone who was undergoing chemotherapy and they had lost all their hair, including eyebrows and eyelashes. Would you blurt out statements about how strange they look? Of course not, your brain would run analysis of the visual data it is receiving and advise you that they must be going through a terrible time. It will suggest you respond with love and compassion rather than ridiculing their appearance.

Due to the filters in our amazing brain we can quickly shift between communication modes, so that we can fit the environment. For example, you probably talk to your parents differently than you do to your best mate. If you met the president of America, the chances are good that you wouldn't get him in a headlock and ruffle his hair. Thankfully, your brain is very good and very quick at making these judgement calls.

Of course if I injected you with a powerful sedative just as you were about to meet the president the story might be quite different. Alcohol interferes with the brain's ability to keep you safe; it doesn't make you brave, confident, funny or relaxed it makes you stupid.

My final word on this is to tell you the story of Ray Thomson (name changed).

Warning: If you are easily offended please skip to the next chapter now. If you choose to read on, be forewarned that I am going to tell you exactly what Ray did and I will use the same inappropriate language he did.

Ray and I worked together many years ago. He is a larger than life character with a great sense of humour and the ability to get the whole room laughing within minutes of his arrival. Unfortunately Ray likes a drink and despite what he thinks, he doesn't get funnier the more he drinks. All that happens is; the filters that prevent Ray's humour crossing the line from cheeky into offensive get deleted. As the night goes on his jokes get ruder and ruder, this is not normally a problem if the people around him are drinking at a similar pace.

One year the media company we were both working for put on a big Christmas party for all sections of the company. The evening was black tie, and people cooing over seeing their office colleagues looking so elegant and smartly dressed took up the first twenty minutes of the party. As usual small talk and polite work related talk dominated the chatter for the first hour. Ray had been holding court and telling gags, while drinking heavily from the free bar.

I first realised Ray had crossed the line when I was standing talking to managing director, a lovely lady called Nicola. She was telling me about how proud she was of her daughter who had just graduated from university. Ray pulled alongside us and started pulling silly faces as we talked. Eventually Nicola turned to him, smiled and asked him what he wanted. I could tell from the glazed over look in his eyes that his response was not going to enhance his career. With a little clear drool clinging to the corner of his mouth, he slurred a response.

"Nicola, I fucking love you... and you have great tits for an older girl"

She handled him well and suggested it was time he went home. I stood there with my jaw on the ground until he staggered away, mumbling equally inappropriate comments. Sadly this was just the beginning of the evening for Ray and he went on to smash a large glass display cabinet in the function room and was eventually forcibly ejected from the hotel for urinating in a potted palm in the reception.

Monday morning at work he was called into a meeting with the Managing Director and the human resources director. He was suspended from work for a month and told to pay for all the damages before profusely apologising to the entire hotel staff.

I am sure you have your own stories about the night a drunken guy caused chaos at a social occasion. If alcohol makes people more sociable then it must do this all the time. As we discussed earlier, alcohol is not a binary liquid that can change it effects depending on the circumstance. If you believe that alcohol does a certain thing, then if it is truly the chemical causing this response logic must dictate that it must always have this effect. Fire is always hot and water is always wet. So why didn't Ray get more sociable when he drank that night?

The answer is simple; every positive state we believe that alcohol creates is a lie. Alcohol is only one thing, an anaesthetic that makes people stupid by interfering with their brain chemistry.

Going back to alcohol is to make a conscious decision to be stupid!

Chapter Four - Everything in moderation

Men are binary animals, and by that I mean they operate in a predominately black and white world. Conversely, women experience life with much more emotion. There is a veritable sea of shades of grey in between those two states of black and white for females. We see this most clearly in the way we are attracted to each other. Men often make snap decisions based on physical appearance. They see a beautiful woman and decide within a millisecond that they would love to have sex with her. Women on the other hand do not operate like this, attraction for a woman is more like a dial than a switch. Her attraction shifts up and down as she gets to know the man, as he ticks specific boxes her interest increases and when he says or does the wrong thing the dial spins back the other way.

"Men are a switch and women are a combination lock"

My father is the very embodiment of this male gender trait. He is a hard working, no nonsense, Northern man who believes nothing is for free and there is no easy short cut to anything in life. When I told him I had stopped drinking and had written a book about it, I explained my concept of the dark magician and how it is not possible to control your drinking and you must stop completely. He looked at me suspiciously and in his dry, confident way he said "nonsense'. I had to laugh, after listening to my one sentence summary of a seventy thousand word book he had analyzed and rejected my concept in one word... 'Nonsense'.

When I asked why he thought the book that had already helped hundreds of other people was nothing more than nonsense. He replied 'it's simple son, everything in moderation, that's the key to a happy life'. ???

My father is wrong, and while saying that still tugs at something deeply ingrained and makes me think I am being slightly disrespectful. I have to accept that the man who I have looked up to since birth is as misguided on this subject as the rest of the western world. The 'everything in moderation' line is one I hear often and it is wielded with such confidence that it will end the debate that it is often a difficult one to argue against.

Apart from the fact, that it is blatantly incorrect. No not everything in moderation... something's are just bad for us and that's the black and white of it. You wouldn't advocate suicide in moderation or depression in moderation. The failing of this 'moderation' standpoint is that it still assumes that there are benefits to drinking an attractively packaged poison, but if you do so in smaller amounts.

Imagine for me that common household bleach was found to have exactly the same effects as alcohol. A little dash of it in a glass of orange juice gave it that same buzz and zing. After a few glasses you felt mellow and happy and a little bit intoxicated.

If you came around to my house and I poured you a freshly squeezed glass of freezing cold orange juice, added some ice and a little fruit on the side. Then I opened the cupboard under the sink where I keep the household cleaning products and squirted a little splash of bleach into the tasty drink... would you drink it?

Of course not, but lets examine the reasons why you wouldn't touch it.

Reason One – I am not drinking that it will kill me!

No it won't the bleach is so diluted that it won't kill you. It may make you feel a little ill and if you drink too much you will probably vomit and need to be put to bed for a while. But does this physical response sound any different to alcohol?

Reason Two – Bleach is a poison, why would I drink it?

Alcohol is also an internationally registered poison. If you go to an chemical supplier and buy a bottle of 100% proof alcohol you will notice that the manufacturer is legally obliged to place the recognized warning symbol for a dangerous poison on the bottle. Emblazoned on the container will be the same ominous skull and crossbones that you see on the side of toilet cleaner. This is no mistake or exaggeration and just because your bottle of booze is give a pretty bottle and called something romantic like 'Rolling Leaf' or "Golden Valley" doesn't detract from the fact that you are drinking diluted poison.

Reason Three – Bleach is a cleaning product, not intended for human consumption.

Bleach is a cleaning product because of what the chemical (normally chlorine) does to microscopic life forms such as bacteria and viruses. If you place some liver cells in a petri dish and examine them under a microscope you will see a uniform array of carefully structured and healthy looking cells. Add a dash of bleach to the sample and what you will witness is pure devastation. The cells will be ripped apart and imploded. Instead of a healthy matrix of cells you will see a jumbled mush of destruction. This specific effect of the chemical means that bleach is perfect for cleaning hospitals, toilets, kitchens and any other areas that are prone to potentially fatal bacteria such as listeria and e-coli.

But guess what, if you add a dash of pure alcohol to the petri dish do you know what the result is?

Exactly the same! At a microcellular level the effects of bleach and alcohol are indistinguishable. So why do you think that adding a dash of cranberry juice turns a lethal poison into a harmless social pleasantry?

The harsh reality is that alcohol is nothing more than poison disguised in pretty bottles with romantic names. Whether alcohol makes food tastes better is a debatable point but the fact that alcohol is a poison is an indisputable point. Nobody can debate that because it would be as pointless as trying to prove that water isn't wet.

In summary, when anyone ever suggests that alcohol can be enjoyed in moderation, please be aware that what they are really saying is poison in moderation is okay. How on earth can it be?

Sorry Dad x

Chapter Five - A refreshing cold beer

Nobody can be better placed to try to understand this belief more than me. These days I live on the Mediterranean island of Cyprus. In the summer, temperatures routinely cross the 100-degree mark (33 degrees centigrade). I must admit for a long time I would sit in the baking sun and scratch my head at why I felt envious of the drinkers with their freezing cold pints of beer. I knew that I didn't want to drink the poison that was in that glass but something was making me want it all the same.

People who claim that beer quenches thirst might as well be claiming gasoline is a suitable substance to extinguish a fire with. Another hard fact about alcohol is that it dehydrates the human body, so it is entirely illogical to insist that if you add a dash of it to a pint of water it suddenly and miraculously becomes more thirst quenching than water on its own.

Back when I was a drinker I had several alarming routines to try and minimize the personal discomfort of drinking attractively package poison on a daily basis.

While I was still sober enough to make sensible choices I would take two giant glasses of water up to the bedroom and place them on the bedside cabinet on my side of the bed. The first was supposed to be downed before I went to sleep, although in truth I was often too intoxicated to remember to do this. The second glass of water was for when I woke in the early hours of the morning with a pounding head and a mouth that felt as dry as the Sahara desert. If alcohol is so refreshing why was this silly routine even necessary.

Don't be so stupid Craig, obviously if you have a skin full then of course you are going to be dehydrated. But one beer really does the trick when you are thirsty.

Again we are back to an assumption that drinking in moderation is somehow a benefit. Alcohol is the waste product of decaying vegetable matter; it is not a NASA designed smart liquid with the ability to change its chemical structure on demand. If ten pints makes you very dehydrated then one pint simply can't have any other effect than dehydrating you to one-tenth the level of the previous example. Expecting anything else to be true would be like assuming the temperature of your bath water will increase if you leave the cold tap running long enough.

Despite this certain knowledge I was still feeling envy around my beer-drinking friends. It was only when I was in a bar in Cyprus with my good friend Mike that I worked out the reason why. It was an unusually hot day and we had both walked two kilometers from the beach and as such were very thirsty. He wanted a pint of the local beer and I was going for a coke. As an experiment I ordered and paid for each drink individually. First a can of coke and a small empty glass were placed in front of me and Andreas the owner of the bar rang up €2.00 on the cash register.

Next I ordered Mike's beer and the experience was significantly different. Andreas reached into the freezer cabinet and pulled out a large, frosted beer pitcher. The ice coated glass glistened in the midday sun and the beer company's logo looked as impressive as a prestigious automobile hood ornament in the center of the thick glass. The goblet was filled with golden beer from the chilled tap and placed on a branded beer mat in front of me. The cash registered displayed €1.75.

Ignoring all the pomp and circumstance of the way the beer was presented. Mike got twice the volume of liquid for less than half the price of my coke. For me to get the same quantity to drink I would need to spend €4.00 to his €1.75. It was at this point that I realized that the whole machine is geared up to encourage us to drink. In bars across the world, the penalty for drinking the non-addictive substance is many fold. If your local bar is charging more for soft drinks than it is for addictive poison, ask yourself why they would do this?

Non-drinkers genuinely consume beverages because they are thirsty. I don't care how hot it gets or how much sport you do, it is highly unlikely that you are going to sit in a bar and drink ten pints of fruit juice. Normally after the first or second drink the body signals that it has had enough fluid and your thirst is quenched. If people really claim they drink pints of lager or beer because they are thirsty then why don't they also stop after the first pint?

The harsh reality is it is scientifically impossible for alcohol to be a good thirst quencher. Alcohol as well as being a registered poison is also a diuretic. This crudely put, means it makes you go to the toilet, a lot! Even at such low concentrations as 4% (as in beer and lager) the alcohol will make you urinate away the total liquid content of the pint glass you have just consumed plus it will pull additional water from your body too. This is why despite having downed ten pints of beer you wake up in the middle of the night with a mouth that feels like a butchers chopping block and you stumble to the fridge to gulp down as much water as possible. It is also why you get a terrible night's sleep as you feel the urge to urinate on an hourly basis. Sometimes when the person is drunk enough they will awake in the morning to find that they have wet the bed. Grown adults reverting to embarrassing childlike behavior because they are choosing to consume a poison for fun.

It is true that over eighty percent of the western world drinks alcohol, but that doesn't make it safe or a sensible thing to do. The fact that 'everyone drinks' and our parents, grandparents and generations as far back as we can recall also drank alcohol, makes us incorrectly believe we are protected by the assumed safety in numbers principle. Actually that is not true, no drinker really believes that he or she is protected because of the social proof around the drug, he or she is just pleased to have another weapon in his or her arsenal to justify their behaviour around a substance that we all inherently know is dangerous and unhealthy.

There is no safety in numbers with alcohol. Just because everyone you know drinks does not make it a safe product, reduce your chances of getting addicted or suffering harm in some way. Whether one person plays Russian roulette or a billion people play the odds remain the same for each person holding the gun. Every pull of the trigger is a separate unique incident and is completely independent of and uninfluenced by all the other triggers being pulled at that time. Just because the people who surround you all appear to be 'in control' of their drinking does not give you licence to assume you will be affected by alcohol in a similar way.

Drinking a poison for fun is nothing short of insane but even insanity looks normal if repeated often enough. Let me give you an example… if I stood in the middle of Trafalgar Square in London dressed as clown, riding around on a tiny child's bicycle. People would quite rightly point and ridicule my behaviour. I would be the unusual freak at the party for all to see. But, if everyone at Trafalgar Square that day was dressed as a clown apart from me, then I would still be consider to be the freak and my behaviour would still be classified as unusual and weird despite the fact that I was the only person being normal.

This is exactly what happens when you stop drinking poison for fun. You are the sane person standing in the asylum and all the inmates are pointing at you and calling you a freak. The good news for you is you can see the insanity for what it is, and walk calmly to the exit and leave it all behind. The drinkers on the other hand can't leave because they don't even know they are in the asylum in the first place.

It is entirely true that you could play Russian roulette for an entire lifetime and never have the gun go off. You would have to be very lucky to get away with that activity but no luckier than to consume a dangerous poison on a daily basis and hope it has no negative repercussions on your life.

If you are frowning at the comparison between a smoking gun and a glass of Whiskey, let me ask you why you are uncomfortable with the analogy? We know that both activities are highly misguided and foolish, we know that both activities will kill you. So the only aspect the people can logically get upset with is a gun kills in seconds and alcohol will take between five and thirty years to do the job.

So would it be fair to say that you are really not concerned with the cause of death and only with the timescale?

Do the rewards of drinking really outweigh the estimated ten to twenty-year reduction in lifespan? Well let's think about that... drinkers have significantly poorer health, are often obese, have less disposable income and are miserable whenever they are not drinking a poison that will eventually kill them. In the cold light of day it really doesn't feel like it is worth giving away up to twenty percent of your life to remain inside the asylum.

Let's put it another way… when I go to the movies I love to get a big bag of sweet and salted popcorn to enjoy as I watch the movie, perhaps you do too? If it was discovered that cinema popcorn was exceptional dangerous and regular consumption knocked twenty years off your lifespan – would you ever buy a bag of popcorn again?

The whole western world has been brainwashed for hundreds of years to believe that alcohol is a benefit. Remember, you are the exception to the rule and that is why it sometimes feels strange to be the only one not drinking. You are the visitor at the asylum and not a patient. For the love of God, do not take advice or criticism off the inmates or you will end up back as one of them

Chapter Seven – Alcohol The Sand Man

Here is an excuse I know only too well, for back when I was a drinker I would claim that I could not get to sleep without a drink or seven inside me. Alcohol is an anesthetic and as such does not induce sleep but rather unconsciousness, which is a very different thing. If you have ever had a general anesthetic or been unfortunate enough to have been knocked unconscious, do you remember coming around and feeling fantastic and well rested? Of course not because sleep is a natural repair and recharge cycle of the human mind and anesthesia merely shuts the brain down.

Back when I was drinking this anesthetic effect of alcohol would mean that I would be out cold and in bed even before my children most nights. My regular bedtime back when I was drinking was eight thirty. I got home from work around six and it took me just two hours to knock myself out. I would lay unconscious in bed for close to ten hours a night and wake up feeling exhausted in the morning, how could this be?

These days I go to bed around midnight and wake feeling amazingly refreshed and well rested just seven hours later. I don't even want to calculate how many precious hours of my life I have chosen to be unaware of. I don't ever want to know about all the cute things my kids did while I was unconscious upstairs and I don't want to even think about the times my family needed me and I wasn't in a fit state to be the man they needed me to be.

This function of alcohol reminds me of a very funny (and at times painfully sad) movie starring Adam Sandler called 'Click'. In which an ambitious architect called Michael Newman, played by Sandler makes a deal with the Devil, whereby he is given a universal remote control that not only does all the usual things you would expect from such a device such as turning on the television or opening the garage doors but in addition it can also magically control real life too. Michael quickly realises to his delight that with the click of a button he can fast forward through time and even skip events all together. He stumbles across this apparently miraculous feature of the remote while shivering in sub zero temperatures waiting for his dog to take a leak before bed. The pooch is quite happy sniffing around the yard, oblivious to the encouragement to 'do his business' coming from his frustrated and freezing owner. Curiously Newman points the remote at the dog and hits the fast forward button. In a blur of activity including the rather repugnant cocking of the leg incident he is left gobsmacked by the awesome power of his new device.

As the story unfolds he uses the remote more and more, skipping arguments with his wife, fast-forwarding boring visits from the in-laws and eventually incorrectly assuming he was shortly to be promoted at work he asks the remote to jump forward to the day he makes partner at his firm of architects. What he doesn't realise is his promotion was actually a whole decade away and the remote is an intelligent device that learns the behaviour of its owner and then attempts to predict future. The remote assumes that because he has skipped such things as sex with his wife, play time with his kids, Christmas and birthday parties that in the future he will also not want to experience them. It then proceeds to ignore his objections and automatically fast forward him through some of the most sacred and special moments in life. Towards the end of the movie we see an aged, ill and overweight Michael Newman who is distraught because he has missed his children growing up, lost his wife to another man and has sold his soul to be the most successful partner in the company. He is desperately unhappy and full of regret at throwing away all the moments that makes life really worth living.

I have watched that movie a dozen times, I must have even seen it four or five times with a big glass of whiskey in my hand completely ~~obvious~~ oblivious to how the universal remote of that same movie serves the exactly same role as alcohol.

Alcohol makes a deal with people but like a shady insurance salesman it fails to tell them about the small print. It promises to make their problems disappear and while it does make good on that deal what it doesn't mention until it is too late is that the problems will be back the next day but much bigger than ever before. And just like a gambling addict desperately chasing his losses looking for one big payday, now the original problems are exponentially bigger and more painful. Unable to cope with the avalanche of worry the drinker must now make another significantly larger deal with the devil – the seemingly unbreakable cycle begins in earnest.

"Alcohol continues to get away with murder. What has long since been banned for all similar, dangerous products, remains FAIR GAME FOR BOOZE." (p.91)

Chapter Eight – The marketing made me do it

Alcohol continues to get away with murder... what has long since been banned for all similar dangerous products remains fair game for booze. Cigarettes were promoted in an equally abhorrent manner until the world woke up to just how damaging they are for health and society in general. The tobacco industry had the Gaul to not only refuse to accept that cigarette smoking caused cancer and a long list of other terrible diseases but they also produced misleading television, radio and press advertisements that hinted that cigarettes enhanced health and life in general.

Towards the back end of the last century the worm started to turn. The United States introduced warning labels on cigarette packages, while this was well intentioned the result was people smoked even more than before. It seems illogical, but when presented with a warning that the thing they were about to do could lead them to an untimely and agonizing death, smokers smoked more!

The reason for this is actually simple. Of course smokers did not want to develop lung cancer, in fact for many it is their worst nightmare. Smokers are not stupid nor are they living with their head buried in the sand like an ostrich. They know that cigarettes are extremely harmful and subconsciously they are very concerned about using them. But all the warnings did was make smokers feel stressed out. And what do smokers turn to when they feel stressed? Yes, that's right they smoke a cigarette.

The tobacco industry made noises about being 'very unhappy' at the warning labels but they soon went quiet when they realized that sales were not declining, actually they were making bumper profits.

what !?

The legislation that really made an impact on the tobacco giants was the ruling in the United States that for every thirty seconds of television time taken up by cigarette companies the TV networks had to give equal time to anti smoking commercials. These advertisements were well made and endorsed by huge celebrities of the time. For the first time the tobacco companies started to notice a decline in sales. They had to find a way to stop these damaging commercials from reaching the viewing and smoking public. The solution they came up with was to appear to fall on their own swords. To offer, supposedly in the interests of the health of the American people to stop advertising their product on television.

Of course the sole reason for this self imposed ban had nothing to do with 'doing the right thing' or any sense of morality, it was simply the only way they could remove the damaging anti smoking advertisements from America's TV screens.

The tidal wave of death from alcoholism has yet to hit us, but make no mistake about it. Exactly as the Titanic was going to hit that iceberg no matter what she did, the rate at which we are consuming alcohol means within a decade we are going see an epidemic of liver disease, alcohol related cancers and pancreatic failure.

Today our supermarkets are bulging at the seams with brand after brand of attractively packaged poison. The manufacturers are relentless in finding more and more substances to hide their drug in. Don't like the bitter taste of beer, no problem have wine. Don't like the acidic taste of wine, no problem have a fruity Alco pop, don't like the sweet taste of Alco pops, no problem have a crème based liquor.

Every taste is catered for. there is no escape. Sweet palettes and savory preferences are all covered; there is no excuse not to drink. This is all before the marketing

93

machine for each individual drinks brand ever rolls out a single advertisement.

In our increasingly litigious world, where you must be able to prove what you say about your product before it can make it to the mass markets, Alcohol is the only product that is free to openly lie about the 'benefits' of its consumption. Red Bull have just been successfully sued by some bright spark in the United States because he claims that their advertising slogan of 'Red Bull: It Gives You Wings' is misleading because it doesn't do anything of the sort. And yet alcohol brands continue to claim such nonsense as their product helps you relax, makes you more attractive to the opposite sex, gives you courage, helps you make friends, raises your social status and even moves you higher up the career totem pole.

The fact that alcoholic drinks manufacturers are still getting away with this, really is like they are raising a single digit to the industry, the advertising watchdogs and even their customers. They are lying to our face with a grin as big as the proverbial Cheshire cat stretched across their fat bloated faces.

Let's take a look at some of the bullshit these companies peddle without any regulation or questioning of their claims.

Stella Artois 'Reassuringly Expensive'

Stella Artois is an export strength premium lager from Belgium. Their expensive and classy marketing chooses to deal with the customers' most likely objection head on. Attempting to turn a negative into a positive. Stella knows that it is not the cheapest beer available and so it tries to position itself as a superior choice. A beer that people with high standards would choose, a hint that consuming their brand of attractively packaged poison places you in a higher social class than people slumming it with the cheaper and presumably inferior beers.

Really? They're having a laugh!

Stella Artois is stronger than most beers available which is probably why its nickname in the United Kingdom is 'wife beater'. Groups of rowdy guys in bars can often be heard jokingly asking their drinking buddies to get them a pint of 'wife beater'. Here is a product that has managed to attract a wholly abhorrent label and yet we laugh about it. The line of what is acceptable has been moved by the drug's parasitic infiltration of everyday life. But

where does the line finally stop. Are we to lower ourselves
eventually to ask for a pint of pedophile, followed by a
drunken roar from our equally inebriated 'friends'.

Reassuringly Expensive is rubbing salt into the wounds
of the millions of people who are failing to care for those
who need it most, because they are spending virtually
every penny they own on a common drug addiction. The
average problem drinker will spend over $125,000 on
alcohol over the space of their drinking career. Many
millions of these people will have at the same time
watched their children grow up in abject poverty without
the basic essentials of life.

Such as Michael I, & when we were children.

When you see the financial destruction that alcohol
addiction causes to hard working families around the
globe you have to assume that a marketing slogan of
reassuringly expensive is some sort of sick joke.

And one more thing Mr. Artois, what exactly is the
advantage of drinking overpriced alcohol? Of one thing
we can be certain is that when their customer lays on the
operating table with liver failure or some other ghastly
illness, the surgeon will not declare the situation to be
not as bad as we expected, because thankfully he was
drinking the expensive stuff'.

The honest slogan for Stella should be 'Stella Artois, we charge more because it does more damage'.

Heineken 'Refreshes the parts that other beers can't reach'.

As we have already discussed, alcohol is a diuretic. It is scientifically impossible for it to be used as an effective solution to hydrate the human body. So why are Heineken still allowed to make this claim?

If tomorrow I started marketing simple cold cream with the slogan 'Beck's Magic Cream... makes you look 20 years younger overnight', how long do you think I would be allowed to continue making such a ridiculous and improvable claim?

And what parts of the body are they actually referring to. Are they suggesting that the human body that has evolved over millions years processes all other liquids one-way and their beer a completely different way. Are they suggesting that when you drink their attractively packaged poison not only do you get a raging headache in the morning but also your toenails hurt?

97

The honest slogan should be 'Heineken dehydrates you the same as other beers do'

Guinness 'Guinness is good for you' ???

This improbable claim was a reference to the iron content of the original recipe for Guinness Irish stout. Whatever the health benefits of the high mineral content of this alcoholic drink were, they were almost certainly rendered irrelevant by the alcohol and the quantity being drunk by the average Irish drinker at the time.

This sort of statement is a bit like claiming that fresh orange juice with a squirt of household bleach is good for you because of the vitamin C content of the OJ.

A more honest slogan should be 'Guinness we doubt you are drinking it for the iron".

St. Pauli Girl 'You never forget your first girl".

St Pauli Girl is a brand of German beer that adorns its bottles with the nostalgic and sexy image of a forces sweetheart.

This marketing slogan is using both sex and nostalgia to try and build an emotional connection with the consumer.

Alcohol is a poison that interferes with and destroys the central nervous system. Alcohol entering the brain via the blood supply has a similar affect to napalm being dropped on a village. The death toll is considerable; millions of cells are destroyed in an instant. So the chances are better than good that you are highly likely to have forgotten the first St. Pauli Girl beer you ever had.

They are also trying to subconsciously link their brand with a sentimental and special memory in your head. Your first girlfriend is likely to be indelibly embedded in your grey matter and the rose tinted glasses that time provide probably means you remember her as being much more attractive and lovely than she actually was.

Alcohol makes men podgy and fat. It causes lipids to collect around the midsection putting a heavy strain on the heart. The constant contamination of the blood with a poison makes blood vessels explode; this is why heavy drinkers have that oh so telling bulbous red nose and

~~blood shot eyes. I would wager that if your first girl saw you now – she would run a mile.~~

A more honest slogan for St. Pauli Girl Beer would be "St Pauli Girl… we help you forget your first girl".

Beck's "Unmistakable German Craftsmanship"

The Germans are famous for attention to detail, especially in their luxury car brands. Mercedes and BMW trade on the craftsmanship of the design team and assembly crew who put each automobile together by hand. Trying to steal this image and apply it to the process of bottling the byproduct of decaying vegetable matter is laughable.

When fruit is left to rot the discharge of this decomposition is alcohol. There is no craftsmanship involved in pumping into the green bottles and sticking a fancy label on the front.

The slogan implies that you are getting something that has been lovingly created. Breathed to life by an artist of impeccable taste and experience. The chances are an old woman in a hairnet pressed a button that squirted the correct amount of brown liquid from a giant vat of the stuff. She probably works this shift for ten hours a day, has done for the last decade and couldn't give a stuff if your beer tastes like the nectar of the Gods or arm pit sweat.

If we apply these stupid labels to non-alcoholic drinks you can instantly see what nonsense they are. Imagine if I opened a carton of orange juice, poured you a glass and then told you to drink it slowly because I had poured it in a very special artistic way that would make it taste amazing. You would quite rightly think I was mad.

Coors 'Brewed with pure Rocky Mountain spring water'

Yes, but with a little squirt of poison too. Everything sounds amazing if you ignore all the bad and only talk about the good.

How would you like a flame grilled fillet steak, served with home cut fries and two of juiciest and tastiest field grown flat mushrooms on the planet. Sounds good right, maybe you can even sense the saliva increasing in your mouth as you imagine cutting into that perfectly cooked steak.

Do you still want it if I tell you that I dropped the steak on the kitchen floor and the dog chewed it up before I could get to it?

Missing information out is just deceptive and wouldn't be allowed with any other product. It would be like cosmetic surgeons claiming there are only benefits to plastic surgery and nothing can go wrong.

NOT SO! Big Pharma Drugs do that as well.

May I suggest instead: Coors 'Poison mixed with really good quality water'.

Don Equis 'Sooner or later you will get it'

We will end this comparison with my favorite Don Equis a Mexican brand of beer that has really gone for the below the belt shot here.

What they are basically saying is if you don't drink our beer it's because you are too thick to understand it.

It implies if you are not currently drinking their beer you are outside the club and when you start you are labeled as one of those refined types who understand what the artists at Don Equis are trying to create.

It's similar to the elitism on display in modern art galleries around the world. As the everyday punter walks up to a pile of garbage on the floor and curls his nose up at what just looks like a mess that any naughty child could have created. Only to feel inferior when the 'art expert' approaches and appears to marvel at the beauty and intelligence of the piece.

Can I suggest a more honest slogan: Don Equis 'It makes you stupid, fat and poor – sooner or later you will get it'.

So yes you see alcohol everywhere but instead of seeing this as something you are missing out on I want you to be aware of the devious and dishonest messages being created by the alcoholic drinks companies. But more important than that, when you look around a bar or party and all the people you see are drinking alcohol, you should be aware that they have all fallen for the bullshit. You may be the only person there who failed to be caught out by the deceptive advertising tricks of the industry.

" Alcohol removes fear by making you too stupid to correctly assess risk. "

Chapter Nine - Alcohol gives me courage

People often say that they feel more confident and brave after they have had a few drinks. Heck there is even a long used saying to explain exactly that effect, you will have no doubt seen nervous grooms being offer a little 'Dutch courage' before making their wedding speech. Perhaps, you may wonder dear reader if there is such a long established label for the said effect that perhaps there could be an ounce of truth in the claim?

The answer I am sure you won't be surprised to hear is no, it is not true. Alcohol does not make people more confident or braver it simply makes them stupid. Bravery by definition is to act in spite of the perception of risk and danger. To run into a burning building to rescue your child or relative is perhaps ill-advised (when considering only your own safety) but it could also be said to be an act of bravery. You are acutely aware of the risk of entering the building, and you know that there is a very good chance you will be badly burned. However, you choose to ignore your fear and act anyway.

This is not the same as when you do something risky while under the influence of alcohol. Alcohol removes fear by making you too stupid to correctly assess risk.

Doing something potentially dangerous without being aware of the risks is not an act of bravery. It is purely the actions of a drunken moron.

Courage can only be present when a person has acted for the greater good having overcome his own fear of the impending event. If you are unaware of the fear then it is not possible to overcome it through pure strength of character.

Confidence is another label that gets incorrectly applied to alcohol. Self-esteem comes from a sense of worth, a deep underlying knowledge of ones value and a belief in your place in society. When was the last time you saw a guy staggering all over the place and thought "wow I wish I was that confident."

Has the shy secretary who at the Christmas party suddenly strips off her clothes and gives the CEO a lap dance suddenly found her self-esteem? Will she wake up in the morning; recall the events of the previous night and smile at how confident she was?

Claiming that alcohol give you confidence is like going to a party in fancy dress and then getting there to discover that you are the only one in the silly costume. You could not claim you were dressing confidently to stand out in a crowd, you simply did not know that everyone else would be dressed in black tie. You don't look confident you just look stupid.

To give you one final example of what I mean, let me take you back nearly twenty years to when I was working at a radio station in Birmingham, England. The managing director was an elegant and suave gentleman by the name of Trevor Nix (name has been changed). Trevor was in his fifties and was a happily married man with two teenage daughters. However, the strong rumor was that he was having an affair with his secretary, the delightful and much younger Margaret. The speculation about their fling was always the hot topic at the water cooler each day. The banter would suddenly stop and awkwardly change to a more innocent line of conversation if Trevor should happen to walk by.

One night in June the station held a charity gala and all the staff were required to attend. We were instructed to schmooze with the guests and make sure they were all having a good time. We were also told we were to stay in attendance until the last guest left, which ended up being around one o clock in the morning. By which time all the guys had had more than their fair share of champagne and cocktails, including me.

As I was feeling so suddenly brave I decided it was time to get the truth about the Margaret rumor. I confidently marched up to Trevor who, very professionally had not touched a drop of booze all night. I slapped him on the back (my first indiscretion) and slurred 'Hey Trev, what's all this about you fucking Margaret in your office after hours'.

I was summoned to the Managing Director's office the next morning and I certainly didn't feel confident or brave as I was lambasted at full volume and warned that if I made any more serious accusations I would be fired without further notice.

That one act of 'confidence' destroyed my working relationship with my manager. I was lucky to secure another job with only a month to run on my existing contract. I had already been told that the company was not planning to renew my employment upon the expiry of my contract.

Drunken people witness such behavior and incorrectly label it as confidence. Alcohol prevents the brain from firing correctly. This is not confidence or anything close to it.

Chapter Ten - Alcohol cheers me up & makes a party go with a swing

A bit like the claims that a cold beer is refreshing, this is another scientifically impossible event. Alcohol is a depressant and its effect on the human mind is cumulative. This means that the more you drink the stronger the depressive action of the poison becomes. So it is literally impossible for alcohol to make people happy.

This of course may be difficult to believe because you will have witnessed many drunken parties that were great fun and everyone seemed extremely happy. Let me assure you that ▌ the joy you observed had nothing to do with the consumption of alcohol. I am certain you will have also attended parties that were dull and boring, and yet they also had plenty of alcohol available. As I mentioned earlier it simply is not possible for alcohol to change its effect at random.

Alcohol is simply the by-product of rotting and decomposing vegetable matter. It is a waste product and nothing more complex or advanced than that. Laughing gas (nitrous oxide) makes people laugh; it does this consistently every time it is inhaled. It doesn't suddenly decide to make some people burp and other people do jumping jacks. The chemical effect of the gas has a certain predictable effect on the human body and that is a constant. If alcohol really has the side-effect of euphoria and happiness then this surely must apply to every application of the drug. Boring parties should be able to be turned into carnivals of fun and frivolity by the pouring of just a few shots of tequila. But we have all witnessed this not to be the case.

Also if alcohol really does have the power to lift mood, why don't hospitals and doctors prescribe it for the poor people who present with clinical depression and other such mental disorders? ???

Essentially you have to see that alcohol is a simple chemical, not a chameleon. What is does to the human body is completely predictable. When you take a pain killer it dulls your headache or sore throat. You don't worry that it might one day do something entirely different.

I am currently on a speaking tour and I am writing this from the comfort of my hotel room in Trafalgar Square, London. This morning I took a stroll through the already busy streets of the city and as I meandered through the speed walking commuters on their way to offices throughout central London I must have passed perhaps a dozen homeless people. A depressing and recurring theme, they were all individually huddled in sleeping bags and wedged against the air-conditioning outlet vents outside stores and offices. They lay soaking up the waste heat being pumped out into the cold October London air. Laying discarded by their makeshift beds are empty half bottles of spirits and crumpled cans of super strength lager.

These people are so trapped in the cycle of alcohol addiction they are now only living to drink. But something is wrong, drinkers insist that alcohol makes a party go with a swing; alcohol makes people who would otherwise be boring becoming fun and happy. Yet I didn't see one homeless person that didn't look anything other than completely destroyed and hopeless. Some looked like they had given up on life, others just looked blank and expressionless but absolutely none of them looked happy!

Here is the reality. Alcohol makes people miserable when they drink it and even more miserable when they can't drink it. A party without alcohol is shunned not because it is boring or that it is impossible to be fun without alcohol. But rather drinkers are miserable when they can't drink!

If you want proof that parties can be fun without alcohol, watch a bunch of eight year olds celebrate one of their birthdays. Watch how they laugh, play and run around with the biggest smiles on their faces. According to the law of the drinker, if we they gave each child a shot of whiskey they would become even happier. Let me assure you that unless you want to get covered in vomit and have to deal with a bunch of crying children this absolutely would not be the outcome. AMEN!

Chapter Eleven - Alcohol 2.0

"The tide and time waits for no man"

Time marches on and with the passage of time comes our emotional and social development as a species. With the progress of time our laws and expectations expand and amplify. There are still shadows of our naïve past littering the legal textbooks of our current generation. There is a law that in the English town of Chester, which sits on the border with Wales that it is legal to kill a Welshman with a bow and arrow if you see him in the town after midnight. This law dates back to a time when battles between the Celts and English raged. The law has simply been forgotten to be repealed and stands there as a testament to our mentality in days gone by. Whether you would actually get away with murder by quoting this law in a courtroom is highly unlikely.

It is not so long back that you could advertise anything you want and make any claim you want. Beauty products promised to remove years from your face overnight, breakfast cereal companies lied about the health giving properties of their sugared flakes and chocolate manufactures got away with claiming that their fattening snacks were actually good for you.

Today you cannot advertise a product with outlandish claims unless you can prove them. What is more, you cannot launch a product for use on or by humans that hasn't been <u>properly tested in expensive clinical trials</u>. (except for Big Pharma and Booze Companies) Even then, if you get it wrong and your product causes harm you are liable for millions of dollars in legal claims.

With this in mind imagine if today I walk into my local patent office and say I would like to register my new beverage and explain I have plans to spend billions of dollars advertising this new drink all over the world. I tell them it is made out of the waste product of rotting vegetables and costs me pennies to produce, but I am looking to charge $30 a bottle for it.

<u>I am asked what the benefits of the product are and I claim</u>: :

- It's makes you happy.
- You are more fun to be around when consuming it.
- It makes you feel brave and courageous.
- It helps you relax and sleep.
- The product makes shy people gregarious.

117

- A good meal is enhanced by its addition to the table.

Of course when asked if I can prove any of these claims I must admit that I can't and mainly because not one of them are true.

I then explain that the product will create the following problems:

- It is highly addictive and people will end up spending money they can't afford to lose on a substance that has no benefits.
- It causes birth defects in unborn babies
- It makes people obese and malnourished at the same time (impressed stuff).
- It destroys internal organs and rips brain cells apart.
- It cause premature aging.
- The morning after drinking the product you will often feel so ill that you won't be able to get out of bed. Consumers will certainly miss several days of work due to the affect of the drink.
- The more of the liquid you drink, the more dehydrated you become.
- It is an anesthetic and puts it's users into a coma.

- If you drink enough of the liquid you will vomit and be extremely ill. Carry on drinking after this point and it will kill you.
- My product will massively increase the number of road traffic accidents.
- And finally it will destroy families, ruin careers and turn promising lives into dust.

Firstly, do you think I would have a hope in hell of getting this product approved for human consumption? Do you think a single supermarket would agree to stock it? Would I last more than a month in business before I got sued to oblivion and back?

If discovered today, Alcohol would be banned before it even saw the light of day. It exists and dominates society so ruthlessly today because it has been around long enough to set it's own precedent. What I mean by that is, the voting majority was already addicted by the time the scientific community; the medical profession and governments discovered just how dangerous it is.

The additional problem we have is the very people who have the power to deal with this product are also addicted. Until very recently in England, the Chancellor of the Exchequer famously delivered his annual budget

119

"If discovered today, alcohol would be banned before it even saw the light of day."

forecast with a large glass of whisky positioned directly on the podium. I am sure one day in the future we will look back and ridicule that the guy in charge of the finances for an entire country chose to deliver his address to the nation while drinking a substance that is proven to make people stupid and clumsy.

Now I want you to consider that list of destruction that alcohol causes and imagine for me that instead of me introducing it as a product available for sale. That instead a terrorist organization such as The Islamic State surreptitiously imported the liquid to our country. Before not too long our communities started to disintegrate and our friends and family started dying by the tens of thousand. Is it not true that once discovered, such an action would be considered an act of war?

If terrorists did to our families what alcohol does we would never stop bombing them. It would be the biggest military action ever recorded in the history of man. And yet we do it to ourselves everyday of the week. What is worse we have all agreed to call it a social pleasantry.

Another common misbelief of the drinker is that alcohol (specifically wine) makes good food taste even better. This would only be possible if alcohol tasted good to begin with, which it doesn't.

Alcohol is a learned addiction, which means you have to force yourself to get addicted. Your body and mind have evolved sufficiently over millions of years to quickly identify alcohol as a poison. It tells you this in clear and uncertain terms. The first taste should be enough to put you off for life, but we watch our friends appearing to enjoy the experience and assume there must be something wrong with us. We wonder why alcohol tastes horrible to us and yet it is pleasant to others, and so we persist. Shortly after our first taste we are given more evidence in the form of hangovers and vomiting – still we push through the growing evidence to force ourselves to get addicted to the drug.

Let's get a clear image in our minds of just how insane this behavior is. If I took you to a fruit tree and told you that the fruit of this particular tree is amazing and you should try it. I actually pressed you further and said that if you didn't eat some fruit I would think you to be a wimp, a social outcast and an abnormal human being. And so you reluctantly agreed to take a bite.

The very moment your teeth pierce the skin of the fruit a bitter and disgusting taste floods your mouth. It tastes vile, even worse than medicine. But remembering my warning you continue eating until you eventually pass out. In the morning you wake up and you feel like you have been run over by a truck. Your head is pounding like a toffee hammer is being continually smashed into you forehead. Your lips are dry and your mouth feel like someone has poured a bag of sand into it. As you attempt to get up from the crumpled mess you have become on the floor your stomach lurches violently and you are sick all over yourself.

With that disturbing image firmly fixed in your mind I now want you to answer me a question:

Would you ever go back and eat from the tree again?

Such an action would be ludicrous wouldn't it? If you kept doing it night after night would you forgive me for being concerned about your mental health and perhaps even having you sectioned (under the mental health act) for your own good?

123

The human mind can be conditioned to believe almost anything. Great and hypnotic orators such as Hitler have proved this on mass. This charismatic leader of the Nazi movement in Germany managed to persuade a whole nation that something so repulsive as mass genocide was not only reasonable but also essential to the safety and security of the people. I am a former clinical hypnotist and I know that given enough time I could convince you that the hot water tap is cold and the cold tap is hot. But can you see that even if I managed to persuade you that this is the case it doesn't actually mean that the water coming out of the hot tap is really cold. It won't stop the water burning you, no matter how strong your convictions are.

Let's agree that alcohol tastes bad and that you have, against all the odds, taught yourself to believe the opposite to be true.

So now let's imagine you have treated you and your partner to an expensive meal at a Michelin starred restaurant. The food has been prepared by one of the most talented chefs in the land using the very finest, locally sourced produce. Every mouthful is a little piece of nirvana exploding over your pallet. So now explain to

Good illustration for Sean

124

me how washing the glorious food down with a foul tasting liquid, made from the waste product of decaying vegetable matter could possibly improve the experience.

If you take something good and add something bad, then, how on earth can it become better as a result? *Good question for the millions of French people who drink wine with every dinner.*

This is breathtakingly illogical and should be seen as nothing more than brainwashing that has been so effectively applied that it has gone beyond the realms of normal human behavior.

One of the 'problems' of my approach to alcohol addiction is that it is so much easier than people expect to stop drinking. While this is most certainly a benefit it is also a handicap to the long-term success of the ex-drinker. After a few months of sober life a lot of the horrid scars of your old drinking life have healed over and faded into the recesses of our memory. We start to forget about all the problems and negative things that alcohol brought into our life on a daily basis and we start to observe people still appearing to have a good time while drinking alcohol. We wonder if 'just one drink' will hurt us and then we start to think that we have the safety net of Craig's books and website. We know that we stopped easily the first time around and assume that to stop again will simply be a repeat reading of the book. This is not always true and let me explain why.

The first time you read 'Alcohol Lied to Me' or took the course at StopDrinkingExpert.com you were desperate to change and all this information was new and exciting. The second time around, the story I tell loses some power because you already know it. Can you imagine going to see a terrifying horror movie and leaving the movie theatre shocked at what you just witnessed on the screen in front of you. Do you think you would be as shocked upon a second viewing of the same movie?

What I am saying to you is I wrote Alcohol Lied to Me Again to give you a second bite at the sober cherry. But there will be no 'Alcohol Lied to Me Yet Again', no third edition. This is your last chance to fix this with my help, if you go back to alcohol after this book you are risking everything. There is always HOPE with God, Mr.Beck

I am sorry to be so harsh about this but I don't want you to be under any illusion of where you are in the process. I expected you to fall off the wagon at some point, that is why this book exists but I want you to know that 'just one drink' is so much more than the small insignificant act that it first appears to be.

What to do next:

If you are still drinking as you read this book then the first thing to do – in the next 24 hours decide when you are going to have your last drink. I want you to drink it and with every sip think deeply about all the negative things it has brought into your life. Imagine how much healthier, wealthier, happier you would be if alcohol had never been introduced to you. If you are overweight, take a grip of the big roll of fat around your waist or thighs and say 'thanks for giving me this alcohol'.

If you have already stopped drinking again, there is no need to have a final drink.

My process of stopping drinking does not require willpower because I hope by now you can see that there are no benefits to alcohol being in your life. However, for two weeks after your last drink you are going to be in a chemical process called 'The Kick'.

'The Kick' is the addictive effect of the drug trying to get you to consume more alcohol. This withdrawal process feels like stress, a general unease and nothing more. It is not painful and there are no physical symptoms – it is all in your head. The reason most people drink at the same time of day (when you get home from work etc.) is because the alcohol kick reaches its climax 24 hours after your last drink. At the very point when you get home from work the drug is applying its maximum pressure on you to drink again. The second a drop of alcohol passes your lips 'The Kick' stopwatch is reset at zero. All the stress and general unease vanish (as a reward for doing as you were told) and you will be left in peace for 24

To which of our children does this apply ???

" At the very point when you get home from work, the drug (alcohol) is applying its maximum pressure on you to drink again. "

hours. You also begin a new 14 day cycle of withdrawal. It doesn't matter if you had gone 2 days or 13 days without a drink, the moment you drink alcohol everything gets reset.

The good news is 'The Kick' from alcohol is very mild and painless. The reason heroin is so difficult to escape from is the utter agony of 'The Heroin Kick'. You must go through a sustained period of unbearable agony while being acutely aware that at any point you can make all the pain go away in less than a second with just one more dose of the drug.

Thankfully alcohol does not put you through that misery and for 14 days, providing you don't drink again, your alcohol withdrawal symptoms will get weaker every day. Over that period and for a few weeks after, the supplements you are now taking (see chapter thirteen for a list) will slowly begin to have a positive effect. They do not work overnight and they work differently for everyone. Some people report a massive improvement within a week, others only notice the impact after a month, and a lot of people are not aware of anything happening until they stop taking them and realize what the supplements were contributing.

If during this period (or at anytime) you get the urge to drink, I want you to use a technique called Thought Field Therapy or TFT. Again, this is a principle that appears to be so simple you can't imagine it providing any tangible benefit.

TFT is an acupuncture technique based on the tapping on specific meridian points in the upper body. A renowned Clinical Psychologist called Roger Callahan discovered the principle of TFT in 1980 when he theorized that all negative thought patterns are actually similar to computer programs that are universally shared by all humans. This is why fear feels the same to me as it does to you, we both run exactly the same programme and so we experience the same physical and mental symptoms of fear accordingly. His system demonstrates that by using unique pressure points in the body we can literally turn off the programme. It's like a CTRL-ALT-DEL option for negative emotions, anxiety, and most importantly in our case, cravings.

The next time you need to turn off your cravings for a drink, find a quiet room, anywhere will do. Using your index and middle finger gently start tapping on your cheek bone, directly under the corner of your eye. Tap between ten and twenty times before repeating the process just above your eyebrow. Keep alternating the meridian point and before each change ask yourself honestly how much you need a drink.

With each series of tapping, give the craving a score out of ten. You may start around the nine or ten level of 'need', but you should find that the number slowly reduces with each sequence. Slowly you will find that your desperation moves from 'must have' to 'like to have' before reaching your goal point of 'I can take it or leave it'.

This step is easily dismissed as new age mumbo jumbo, but I don't need you to take my word for it, a quick

Thought Field Therapy ?!?

Google search for evidence of Thought Field Therapy success will show you how successful this technique has been for thousands, if not hundreds of thousands, of other people just like you. There are also plenty of videos showing you how to use this technique at my website.

During the kick you may experience a few strange sensations. It is highly likely you will dream about drinking alcohol, this is not because you want to drink, but rather a reflection of what is top of your priority list at the moment. Obviously you are addressing alcohol as a problem in your life, and so your dreams are built around your current focus. This is why after watching a movie you can sometimes dream a similar plotline to what you have just seen, but with yourself playing the role of the protagonist.

When I stopped drinking I would often wake in the morning feeling absolutely convinced I had been drinking heavily the night before, sometimes the dreams were so vivid I would check the garbage for alcohol bottles. Don't be afraid or question the significance of these dreams, as with everything else you observe, simply smile and acknowledge them. These dreams are a good sign, they are evidence that you are going through exactly the same series of events that I did, and the end result of that is a complete repulsion to the thought of drinking another alcoholic drink.

Mrs Booze is dying (or is it Mr. Booze)

Another slightly strange thing to expect is dealing with a slight sense of loss when in situations where you would have previously consumed alcohol. Don't worry this is will also fade over time as the neural pathways in your brain dedicated to drinking weaken and erode.

Alcohol addiction is similar to getting stuck in quicksand. In both cases, we make an inaccurate assessment of the risk and the situation. We tend to only address our drinking when we have already started sinking up to our waist. You will notice that in areas where quicksand is a possibility they do not put up the warning signs in the middle of the danger. They put them right out there on the perimeter, long before you get near the danger zone.

The same is true of alcohol. When you first take a sip of booze and discover to your shock that it tastes vile. This should be an alarm bell that scares us off for life. However, we take a look around and notice that everyone else is drinking and apparently enjoying their alcoholic drink. So we persevere despite all the evidence suggesting that drinking horrible tasting poison for fun is at best ill-advised.

So, we learn how to tolerate alcohol and to mix our metaphors, we keep walking towards the center of the quicksand. Then, when we realize we are sinking, we start to panic and struggle to control our drinking. We use willpower to force ourselves to drink less of the thing we want most in the world. The truth is using willpower to escape an alcohol problem is as misguided a plan as kicking and struggling are as an effective way to get out of quicksand.

The harsh reality is the more you panic the deeper you sink. The more you try to force yourself to go back to being a 'normal or social' drinker of attractively packaged poison the more you experience failure. Constantly failing to achieve your goal leads to low mood and stress. This then accelerates the problem because us drinkers have a solution for times when we are a bit down in the dumps... we drink!

It's very hard to get out of quicksand on your own. Really what you need is someone to come along, spot you are in trouble and reach out a hand to help you out. That is exactly what I do for people like you!

This book is a powerful first step because not least, you have taken action on a problem that the vast majority of people refuse to deal with. However, if you are otherwise a successful individual with a lot to lose then refusing to take that helping hand is a gamble with significant consequences.

Consider what could happen to your career, income, reputation and loved ones if you don't deal with this problem. How would life look like in five years time if your drinking just kept getting worse? To which of our children does this apply, along with you, Sean?

Helping people escape the trap of alcoholism is my passion. If you ever attend one of my quit drinking events you will see just how much I throw into this. I live it and I breathe it. This is why over the years I have gained the reputation as the World's #1 Quit Drinking Mentor. Every year I work with a handful of people on a one to one basis. I effectively become your sponsor. We talk (video) on a regular basis and I make sure you nail this problem once and for all.

This is the most powerful and effective alcohol cessation solution anywhere today.

- Personal mentor calls with Craig Beck
- Custom scripted & recorded hypnosis
- Complete step by step video course
- Secret Facebook group
- Inner circle upgrade
- Non-judgmental community
- Free entry into any live event
- 75 hours video & audio coaching
- 90 days intensive support
- Lifetime access & support

If you are interested in my Executive Quit Drinking Program visit the website and arrange a free consultation with me.

Chapter Fifteen – Supplements & Closing Words

Firstly, stop drinking, I mean today... right now. Unlike before when you have had this brave moment we are going to do something vitally different, we are going to stop the first imbalance from triggering the second imbalance. Remember, for the next two weeks you may feel uneasy, uncomfortable and anxious, this is caused by the kick from alcohol, an addictive drug. The good news is once you get 14 to 15 days sober, the symptoms are so mild you can't distinguish them from the genuine emotions of daily life. Really ???

This time when you quit we are not going to leave you at the mercy of your imbalanced brain chemistry. We know one of the most important substances for proper brain function, and by that I mean having correctly functioning neuro transmitters and receptors, is essential fats in the brain. If you have ever spilt oil or fat on a piece of fabric you will know that water won't even touch it. To get rid of an oil stain you need to add a chemical solvent to break it down. You won't be surprised to hear that one solvent that is particularly good at this job is alcohol. While this is good news if you need to rescue an expensive sofa with a nasty oil stain, it is very bad news for us problem drinkers. Alcohol destroys essential fat; it rips through it like napalm.

As a heavy drinker you almost certainly have an essential fat deficiency, and this means your receptors cannot function correctly. This problem means that when your body creates the dopamine and serotonin that make you feel good; you are going to struggle to absorb them at a sufficient level to be noticeable.

Can you now see that if you understand the truth about alcohol, are free of the kick and feel great within yourself (because the dopamine and serotonin is pumping naturally around your body), there is very little chance you will even want to drink, and so you don't. If you have given up the drink but feel terrible and depressed you are obviously more likely to assume it is the alcohol that was making life bearable and return to it as a solution to your problem.

The two specific essential fats that we need to take onboard at the point where we stop drinking are Eicosapentaenoic Acid and Docosahexaenoic Acid. Known better simply as EHA and DHA, and you can find both these in a high quality Omega 3 supplement. Go to your local health store and buy a 1000MG Omega 3 fish oil supplement and take three of these a day, either all at once or spread over the day. Do not buy cod liver oil tablets as they contain a large amount of vitamin A, which may combine with some of the other supplements I am going to ask you to take and cause some rather unpleasant side effects.

It's important that you follow this method to the letter; I understand there is a cost involved with buying high quality supplements, but I promise you it will be significantly less than you are currently spending on alcohol. Do not be tempted to remove any of the recommended steps or supplements from the method (unless you have an underlying medical condition that warrants such a precaution); they are all-effective and work exceptional well together to create our desired outcome of permanent sobriety.

In some recent research, two dozen mice were deliberately given alcohol until they became dependent upon it. From this point on they were allowed to have as much or as little alcohol as they wanted, and their consumption was monitored. Twelve of the mice were removed from the testing area and fed high strength Omega 3 before being placed back into the test. Despite alcohol being freely available, the twelve mice treated with Omega 3 consumed significantly less alcohol than the untreated animals. Omega 3 is so effective because EPA actually repairs parts of the brain damaged by alcohol. It balances your moods and emotions, plus it's very good for your heart too. DHA is used directly as a material to rebuild brain tissue damaged by the years of napalm you have fired into your brain.

Next, we are going to work on your production of important 'feel good' neuro chemicals. To create healthy amounts of serotonin, melatonin and dopamine, your body and brain need the raw materials that come directly from external sources (they cannot be created independently). Normally you would get enough of these elements from your food (if you were eating a healthy and balanced diet), but we are starting with a handicap, effectively we are trying to start a car with a flat battery on a cold morning. So when you are in the health food store buying your Omega 3, I want you to also buy a good quality multivitamin, it absolutely must contain a decent level of vitamin C, magnesium and zinc. Virtually all high street multivitamins will contain vitamin C, but only the comprehensive A to Z brands will contain the full range of elements. Additionally I would advise you to further increase your intake of vitamin C by eating significantly more citrus fruits, or by adding another supplement of ascorbic acid.

see Bio Care

The multivitamin is like a broadsword covering most of your needs up to somewhere near the RDA amount.

However, as problem drinkers we are not your average human beings, we need some of the vitamins and minerals in significantly higher dosages than the standard individual. So please also add to your health store shopping basket a once a day B vitamin complex.

All the supplements we have talked about so far are designed to repair the damage done by years of alcohol abuse and ensure the important parts of our brain have the tools they need to work to peak efficiency. The final piece of the supplement jigsaw comes with the amino acid needed to create Serotonin. If you are deficient in this neuro transmitter you can't help but feel depressed. As a problem drinker you are highly likely to be low on this vital chemical.

If you have been consuming an unhealthy amount of alcohol (not that there is a healthy amount) for a significant period of time your brain and body will have already adapted to the new (unhealthy) reality you have created. It's this power of human adaptability that is often underestimated and provides a convenient smoke screen to the problem that lies hidden beneath. If people dropped down dead after a week of heavy drinking do you think the current worldwide epidemic of alcoholism would exist?

There is a famous story of an elderly man who had given a pint of blood once a month for nearly forty years of his life. Eventually the time came where the blood bank advised him that his blood was no longer suitable for donation and while they were very grateful for his years of generosity they could no longer use his blood for medical purposes. The gentleman stopped making his monthly trip to the donation center and it wasn't long before he started to feel very ill. He repeatedly visited his GP complaining of vague symptoms of unease and generally feeling uncomfortable. It took quite sometime before they were able to establish that he simply had too much blood in his system. His body had adapted to losing at least a pint of blood every month without fail. He had become conditioned to producing blood at a rate to compensate and only when the situation changed the adaptation became noticeable.

You have adapted to poison being present in your system and when you stop drinking you may become aware of this adaptation for the first time. This feeling of unease is not caused by the loss of alcohol but rather it is a clear indication of what your body has had to do in order to keep you alive in such a polluted lifestyle. When you quit the booze your brain chemistry will once again be out of balance for a while until it readapts to life as it is supposed to be lived. The method is all about taking the struggle and pain out of giving up drinking so its important that we take some supplements to ensure we don't have to deal with a low mental state during the kick period.

The production of Serotonin is a two-part process that begins in the gut and is completed in the brain. This is a crucial component of my stop drinking method, and can only be created by consuming an amino acid called tryptophan, which is found in turkey, soy beans, tuna, halibut and other fish. The easiest way for us to get the correct amount of tryptophan is to take a supplement called 5-HTP, which stands for 5-Hydroxytryptophan. You need to take two 50MG capsules about 30 minutes before bed with a small sugary drink. This could be a mug of hot chocolate or even just a piece of chocolate if you prefer.

The reason for this specific 5-HTP ritual is this amino acid is transported to the brain by insulin, which is created by the pancreas as a reaction to consuming sugar. If there is plenty of insulin rushing around your system, the 5-HTP will reach its target quicker and more effectively (of course if you are diabetic you should skip this step). We take this supplement last thing at night because the brain converts serotonin into melatonin, which calms our mind and prepares us for the sleep cycle. So, a pleasant side effect of more Serotonin 'happy chemicals' is a better sleep pattern. After a fairly short period of time you should notice that you find it easier to get to sleep and feel more rested when you awake in the morning.

Because of the potential for side effects and interactions with medications, you should take dietary supplements only under the supervision of your health care provider.

Tryptophan use has been associated with the development of serious conditions, such as liver and brain toxicity, and with eosinophilic myalgia syndrome (EMS), a potentially fatal disorder that affects the skin, blood, muscles, and organs (see "Overview" section). Such reports prompted the FDA to ban the sale of all tryptophan supplements in 1989. As with tryptophan, EMS has been reported in 10 people taking 5-HTP.

Side effects of 5-HTP are generally mild and may include nausea, heartburn, gas, feelings of fullness, and rumbling sensations in some people. At high doses, it is possible that serotonin syndrome, a dangerous condition caused by too much serotonin in the body, could develop. Always talk to your health care provider before taking higher-than-recommended doses.

People with high blood pressure or diabetes should talk to their doctor before taking 5-HTP.

If you take antidepressants, you should not take 5-HTP.

People with liver disease, pregnant women, and women who are breastfeeding should not take 5-HTP.

If you are currently being treated with any of the following medications, you should not use 5-HTP without first talking to your health care provider.

Antidepressants -- People who are taking antidepressant medications should not take 5-HTP without their health care provider's supervision. These medications could combine with 5-HTP to cause serotonin syndrome, a dangerous condition involving mental changes, hot flashes, rapidly fluctuating blood pressure and heart rate, and possibly coma. Some antidepressant medications that can interact with 5-HTP include:

- SSRIs: Citalopram (Celexa), escitalopram (Lexapro), fluvoxamine (Luvox), paroxetine (Paxil), fluoxetine (Prozac), sertraline (Zoloft)
- Tricyclics: Amitriptyline (Elavil), nortryptyline (Pamelor), imipramine (Tofranil)

149

- Monoamine oxidase inhibitors (MAOIs): Phenelzine, (Nardil), tranylcypromine (Parnate)
- Nefazodone (Serzone)

Carbidopa -- Taking 5-HTP with carbidopa, a medication used to treat Parkinson's disease, may cause a scleroderma-like illness. Scleroderma is a condition where the skin becomes hard, thick, and inflamed.

Tramadol (Ultram) -- Tramadol, used for pain relief and sometimes prescribed for people with fibromyalgia, may raise serotonin levels too much if taken with 5-HTP. Serotonin syndrome has been reported in some people taking the two together.

Dextromethorphan (Robitussin DM, and others) -- Taking 5-HTP with dextromethorphan, found in cough syrups, may cause serotonin levels to increase to dangerous levels, a condition called serotonin syndrome.

Meperidine (Demerol) -- Taking 5-HTP with Demerol may cause serotonin levels to increase to dangerous levels, a condition called serotonin syndrome.

Triptans (used to treat migraines) -- 5-HTP can increase the risk of side effects, including serotonin syndrome, when taken with these medications:

- Naratriptan (Amerge)
- Rizatriptan (Maxalt)
- Sumatriptan (Imitrex)
- Zolmitriptan (Zomig)

You may also hear stories that 5-HTP causes heart valve damage in laboratory mice. This is slightly erroneous information and there are some rather tenuous assumptions being made to reach that particular theory. While it is true that injected serotonin does create a small risk of heart valve disease in scientific animals, the same does not appear to apply to orally ingested serotonin.

However, that said and with all supplements, if you have any reason to be concerned (such as a pre-existing heart condition), you are advised to ask your doctors advice before starting on any supplement.

B Vitamins

Vitamin B12 is a water-soluble vitamin that keeps your nerves and red blood cells healthy. It is responsible for the smooth functioning of several critical body processes.

It is possible for the body to develop a vitamin B12 deficiency. This deficiency is usually reported with symptoms of fatigue. As you can imagine the last thing you need when trying to stop drinking is a lack of energy.

Strict vegetarians, heavy drinkers and smokers, pregnant and breast-feeding women, and the elderly usually require vitamin B12 supplements. Sometimes our body, mainly our digestive system, is not able to absorb this vitamin well. This can happen when a person has pernicious anemia, celiac disease, Crohn's disease, bacteria growth in the small intestine, or a parasite.

A deficiency in vitamin B12 can result in a host of illnesses like anemia, fatigue, weakness, constipation, loss of appetite, weight loss, depression, poor memory, soreness of the mouth, asthma, vision problems, and a low sperm count.

The top 5 health benefits of vitamin B 12 are:

• It is needed to convert carbohydrates into glucose in the body, thus leading to energy production and a decrease in fatigue and lethargy in the body.
• B12 helps in healthy regulation of the nervous system, reducing depression, stress, and brain shrinkage.

• It helps maintain a healthy digestive system. Vitamin B12 also protects against heart disease by curbing and improving unhealthy cholesterol levels, protecting against stroke, and high blood pressure.

• B12 is essential for healthy skin, hair, and nails. It helps in cell reproduction and constant renewal of the skin.

• Vitamin B 12 helps protect against cancers including breast, colon, lung, and prostrate cancer.

Yet again your daily multivitamin is not going to cut it. If you are anything like me (back when I was a drinker) you may have been abusing your body for a long time with alcohol. I take an additional B Vitamin complex on top of my multivitamin and having read the possible results of being deficient in this area I am sure you can see why it is an important addition to your own daily routine.

Vitamin D

There is a pandemic of Vitamin D deficiency that is causing ill health; lethargy and weight gain around the world. The problem has been created by our modern lifestyle choices, increased alcohol consumption, several key incorrect assumptions and the cutthroat dollars and cents mentality behind our medical research techniques.

A deficiency in Vitamin D has been linked to diseases from Dementia, Chron's and Cancer to the repeated appearance of the common cold and flu.

I have witnessed the effects of Vitamin D deficiency first hand. A few years ago my daughter Aoife started to complain about pain in her bones and skin. She also started to get random and volatile swings in mood and behavior. As she was just entering that difficult phase of life that involves leaving childhood behind and becoming a teenager, as such we initially put these symptoms down to growing pains and the sort of general teenage moodiness all kids go through.

However, the symptoms slowly got worse and worse until she was taking an unhealthy amount of pain relief just to get through each day. The doctors initially assumed an auto-immune disorder was most likely, as her mother had already been diagnosed with Lupus (SLE). Thankfully the blood test was negative for the SLE markers and all the other serious conditions they checked her for.

Coincidently this was around the time I was starting to research Vitamin D and Magnesium and it struck me that a lot of the symptoms I was reading about sounded very similar to what Aoife was complaining about. I suggested to the doctor that we test for these two elements. The magnesium test came back first and it showed no problem but a few days later we got a telephone call to say Aoife was severely Vitamin D deficient and they were going to prescribe a daily supplement.

As most people know the best source of Vitamin D are the UV rays of the sun. These rays stimulate a process in the skin that creates an inactive form of the vitamin. The liver then converts this inert substance into a powerful and vital element that is important to health and longevity. The problem is, over the last century our lifestyles have changed faster and more profoundly than in any period before. Human beings in the past have been predominately outdoor, manual workers until relatively recently in our evolution.

Agricultural and industrial work dominated until the information age came along. We no longer work the fields but rather tend to sit in front of a computer monitor all day long before going home to then sit in front of a bigger screen until bedtime. Children no longer play games in the streets and climb trees for fun. You are much more likely to see them sitting in front of a games console killing Zombies with an AK47 (unaware of the irony that they look a bit like zombies themselves).

False Assumption One:

We can get all the Vitamin D we need from a few minutes sunshine each day.

This is not true as the assumption is too broad. That theory might be perfectly adequate when applied to fair skinned people living near or on the equator of the earth. However, several factors will mean that it is an ineffective solution to virtually all other people.

• The darker your skin the less well you create Vitamin D.

• The strength of the UV rays dramatically decreases the further north of the equator you go.

• We have slowly become terrified of the sun and now routinely apply sunscreen to ourselves and our children as part of our daily routine.

• A sunscreen with a sun protection factor of 8+ will block over 96% of the UV rays needed by your skin to produce vitamin D.

Not only are we most employed on an indoor basis but also many people now choose to eat their lunch in front of their workstation. The concept of a lunch hour has been eroded by career ambitions and the financial climate.

The reality is that our lifestyles have slowly changed and moved us out of the sunlight. It will be several hundred thousand years before evolution catches up. So you can either wait or start taking a supplement – your choice!

False Assumption Two:

Vitamin D is just another vitamin and no more important that any of the others.

Our blasé approach to supplements causes a problem here because it fails to give Vitamin D the spotlight it deserves. Actually the problem is more to do with the label, Vitamin D is not actually a vitamin but rather it is an essential hormone.

A hormone is a substance that is produced in one part of the body but has a wide-ranging effect on various other important parts of the body such as the brain, heart and other vital organs.

Vitamin D is so much more than a vitamin, it is as essential to good health as sleep, food and exercise.

False Assumption Three:

If Vitamin D was the solution to all the problems mentioned then surely my doctor would test for it and recommend it as an effective treatment.

The reality is that you are most likely to have never been tested for Vitamin D deficiency and here is the reason why:

Vitamin D fails to make it onto the medical training agenda and into doctor's surgeries due to the dollars and cents mentality of our medical research. Pharmaceutical companies do not strive for a cure for cancer because they are lovely caring people with a determination to see us all live a long and healthy life but rather the truth is; developing and then monopolizing a cure for a serious disease or illness means massive profits for their shareholders. Vitamin D is inexpensive and freely available around the world, over the counter and without prescription and therefore it is worthless to the medical research companies out to invent the next miracle cure. Sadly most of the information fed into our doctors and medical training facilities still comes directly from the major pharmaceutical companies.

Thank you Mr. Beck !!!

Combine this selective hearing of the medical community with the out of date information still being peddled by governments who are still quoting dosage information long since out of date and you have Vitamin D left sitting on the shelf.

Vitamin D and Weight Loss:

On top of all the other health benefits of Vitamin D there is an interesting side effect that is weight reduction (or perhaps a better phrase would be weight correction). I am not suggesting taking a D supplement for this reason alone but it is a pleasant added bonus to what I consider to be a true miracle addition to any diet.

There are a lot of empty calories in alcohol and I am sure my unhealthy consumption of a daily bottle of wine added to the extra 60lbs of fat I was also carrying around. So for many people hooked on booze and looking to stop there is an additional bonus in the potential weight loss they will see as a result of their actions. There have been several studies that have linked vitamin D to weight loss.

Vitamin D has been shown to be very effective in increasing the amount of body fat loss while increasing your energy levels at the same time. By increasing your energy levels, the body can overcome chronic fatigue and lethargic moods.

One of the latest research studies conducted by the University of Minnesota discovered that people with weight problems would have more success in losing weight if their vitamin D levels are increased to a higher level. The lead researcher, Dr. Shalamar Sibley, found solid evidence that out of 38 obese men and women, the people that had a higher vitamin D level were able to lose more weight than those who had a lower level of vitamin D.

So how much do you take?

Again I will remind you that I am not a doctor and you must do your own research before taking any of the supplements. All I can do here is tell you what I personally take and explain why I do so.

The 'out of date' recommended daily allowance for Vitamin D, and what you will most likely see quoted on the side of your multivitamin bottle is 200 iu per day. When I discovered what the leading experts in this field are now recommending I was blown away by just how inaccurate the government official RDA is.

Vitamin D can be taken monthly, weekly or daily. Personally I just add it as part of my morning routine, that way I can keep a close eye on what I am doing and how it is affecting me. I recommend adding a vitamin D supplement to your diet at an amount of 20 iu per pound of body weight. For example, I weigh in at 192 lbs and so I take 3900 iu per day. You can expect to see noticeable improvements in health, mobility and weight between two weeks and three months after starting supplementation.

If you are interested in reading more about the Vitamin D pandemic and why this hormone is so vital and yet so over looked then please read:

The Vitamin D Cure by James Dowd

The Power of Vitamin D by Sarfraz Zaidi

Other Essential Supplements

Vitamin K2

There is a delicate balance between Vitamin D and K2. It is vital that if you are supplementing your diet with high strength Vitamin D that you also take a daily Vitamin K2 tablet.

Magnesium

Another vital element that goes hand in hand with your Vitamin D supplementation is the mineral magnesium.

Magnesium is an essential mineral for staying healthy and is required for more than 300 biochemical reactions in the body. Multiple health benefits of magnesium include transmission of nerve impulses, body temperature regulation, detoxification, energy production, and the formation of healthy bones and teeth.

Health specialists have always emphasized the importance of including adequate amounts of vitamins and minerals in our daily diet. Zinc, calcium, and magnesium are three of the most important minerals essential for good health. Magnesium aids in the absorption of calcium by the body, while zinc actively supports the body's immune system.

Women of all ages benefit immensely from the intake of magnesium. Besides keeping osteoporosis at bay, magnesium health benefits in women include relief from symptoms of menopause and premenstrual syndrome (PMS). It also minimizes the risk of premature labor.

The other crucial health benefits of magnesium include protein synthesis, relief from bronchospasm (constricted airways) in the lungs, and improvement of parathyroid function. It boosts the bio-availability of vitamin B6 and cholesterol, improves muscle functioning, and prevents osteoporosis, insomnia, constipation, heart attacks, hypertension, migraines, kidney stones, and gallstones.

Good dietary sources of magnesium include nuts (especially almonds), whole grains, wheat germ, fish, and green leafy vegetables. As with most nutrients, daily needs for magnesium cannot be met from food alone which is why magnesium dietary supplements are recommended as well.

The top five health benefits of magnesium are:

1. Magnesium may reverse osteoporosis

Multiple research studies conducted have suggested that calcium supplemented with magnesium improves bone mineral density. Magnesium deficiency alters calcium metabolism and the hormones that regulate calcium, resulting in osteoporosis. Intake of recommended levels of magnesium is important because it averts osteoporosis.

2. Magnesium prevents cardiovascular diseases

One of the most important benefits of magnesium is that it is associated with lowering the risk of coronary heart diseases. Dietary surveys have suggested that sufficient magnesium intake may reduce the chance of having a stroke. Magnesium deficiency increases the risk of abnormal heart rhythms, which increases the risk of complications after a heart attack. Therefore, consuming recommended amounts of magnesium dietary supplements may be beneficial to the cardiovascular system.

3. Magnesium regulates high blood pressure

Magnesium plays a key role in regulating blood pressure naturally. Magnesium supplements and a diet including plenty of fruits and vegetables, which are good sources of potassium and magnesium, are consistently associated with lowering blood pressure.

4. Magnesium treats diabetes

Studies show that individuals with a magnesium deficiency have a risk of developing type-2 diabetes and severe diabetic retinopathy. Magnesium aids in carbohydrate metabolism and influences the release and activity of insulin, thereby controlling blood glucose levels. It has been proven that for every 100 milligrams of increase in magnesium daily intake, there was a 15 percent decrease in the risk of developing type-2 diabetes.

5. Magnesium treats migraines, insomnia, & depression

The numerous magnesium health benefits also include the treatment of migraines, insomnia, and symptoms of depression. Magnesium is also known to cure severe forms of psychiatric dysfunctions including panic attacks, stress, anxiety, and undue agitations. Magnesium supplements considerably reduce the severity of such attacks and may also help in reducing the rate of recurrence.

Finally I would like to thank you for reading Alcohol Lied to Me Again... don't feel bad that you are back here again but make sure you never return. It may seem strange for an author who makes his living from selling books to say this but I sincerely hope I never see you again. Well, at least in the context of being an unhappy drinker of poison.

Remember that despite all the pretty bottles and devious advertising that is all alcohols is... poison. Life is a precious gift that is beautiful but shockingly short – don't let the dark magician steal one more second, one more relationship or one more vital cell of your amazing and perfect body.

If you need some extra support or have a specific question please come see me at

www.StopDrinkingExpert.com

If you have enjoyed this book would you mind writing me an honest review at the online store you bought it from? I always read them and they always mean a lot to me (good or bad).

Your Ex-Drinking Friend

Craig Beck

The Stop Drinking Expert

Recommended links
- https://www.CraigBeck.com
- https://www.StopDrinkingExpert.com

Follow Craig Beck on Social Media
- Facebook: https://www.facebook.com/craigbeckbooks
- Twitter: http://twitter.com/CraigBeck

Download the total control alcohol course as soon as you join

Why not decide now and start to feel the benefits within 24 hours of joining

7 Life changing aspects to joining today

1. Significantly more effective than cold turkey or willpower methods.

2. 100% private & confidential solution – completely online process.

3. Protects your career – no need to take time off work to attend therapy.

4. Personal support from best selling author and ex-drinker Craig Beck.

5. No prescription drugs – no medication with problematic side effects.

6. Save thousands – the average Stop Drinking Expert member saves over $3000 per year.

7. Repair relationships – become a better parent, partner and friend.

I have been where you are...

Why you should believe me on this?... I am not a doctor telling you to drink less, I know it's not that easy!

My program works so well because I have been in the same alcohol-trap as you and escaped... Two bottles of wine a night and even more at the weekends was normal for me.

I know you don't want to stand up and call yourself an alcoholic. Actually I don't believe you are, as soon as you get started I will tell you exactly why this is the case.

100% private solution

I understand you don't want to risk your career or have any sign of this problem on your medical records. With my online stop drinking cure, you can deal with this in 100% privacy.

Another of the things you are going to love about my control alcohol system is you will be able to cut down or even how to quit drinking completely

When you get started today and join the thousands of other who are back in control of their drinking.

www.stopdrinkingexpert.com

" CONFIDENCE is another label that gets incorrectly applied to alcohol. Self-esteem comes from a sense of worth, a deep underlying knowledge of our value, and a belief in our place in society. When was the last time you saw a guy/woman staggering all over the place and thought: " WOW!!! I wish I was that confident !!! "   (p. 106)

" Here is the reality: Alcohol makes people miserable when they drink it, and even more miserable when they can't drink it. A PARTY WITHOUT ALCOHOL is shunned NOT BECAUSE it is boring or that it is impossible to BE FUN without alcohol. BUT RATHER : Drinkers are miserable when they can't drink. " (p.114)

18331235R00102

Printed in Great Britain
by Amazon